SCRIPTURE THERAPY™
DAILY DEVOTIONAL
for MEN

Effective Help for Men in Conquering Life's Difficult and Challenging Issues

BENJAMIN OPALEYE

Scripture Therapy Daily Devotional for Men

Published in Great Britain in 2014 by Scripture Therapy Resources Ltd,
P. O. Box 68475,
London N16 1EJ
UK

www.ScriptureTherapy.com

Text and illustrations Copyright © Benjamin Opaleye, 2014

The right of Benjamin Opaleye to be identified as the author and illustrator of this work has been asserted in accordance with the Copyright, Design and Patents Act, 1988.

All rights reserved. This book or parts thereof may not be copied, reproduced, stored in a retrieval system, or transmitted in any form by any means-electronic, mechanical, photocopy, recording, or otherwise without prior written permission of the publisher.

The intent of this book is to provide accurately quoted scriptures from various versions of the Bible. It is sold with the understanding that the publisher and author are not attempting to render advice, prescriptions, psychological, financial, legal, or other professional services. If expert assistance or counselling is needed, the services of an appropriate professional should be sought.

Scripture quotations marked (GNB) are taken from the Good News Bible © 1994 published by the Bible Societies/HarperCollins Publishers Ltd., UK Good News Bible © American Bible Society 1966, 1971, 1976, 1992, Used with permission.

Scripture quotations marked (CEV) are from the Contemporary English Version © American Bible Society 1991, 1992, 1995. Used by permission/Anglicisations © British & Foreign Bible Society 1997.

Scripture quotations marked (AMP) are taken from the AMPLIFIED BIBLE. Copyright © 1954, 1958, 1962, 1964, 1965, 1987 by The Lockman Foundation. All rights reserved. Used by permission. (www.Lockman.org)

British Library Cataloguing in Publication Data.
A catalogue record for this book is available from the British Library.

ISBN: 978-0-9576826-4-1

Printed and bound in Great Britain

Dedication

This book is dedicated to every person desiring to experience a happier, healthier, more fulfilling life. May you always find strength and wisdom from the scriptures to overcome life's every challenge.

—Benjamin Opaleye

"Everything in the Scriptures is God's Word. All of it is useful for teaching and helping people and for correcting them and showing them how to live."
— II Timothy 3:16 (CEV)

Contents

Preface 11
How to get the Most out of This Devotional 12

Chapter 1
Scripture Therapy To Help Men Conquer
FAMILY ISSUES 15

1a) Protection Over You and Your Family Members 16
Read On: January 1st | March 18th | June 3rd | August 19th | November 4th

1b) Maintaining Peace and Harmony at Home 18
Read On: January 2nd | March 19th | June 4th | August 20th | November 5th

1c) Keeping A Healthy Parent-Child Relationship 20
Read On: January 3rd | March 20th | June 5th | August 21st | November 6th

1d) Showing Love to Your Family Members 22
Read On: January 4th | March 21st | June 6th | August 22nd | November 7th

1e) Controlling Your Temper When Family Upset You 24
Read On: January 5th | March 22nd | June 7th | August 23rd | November 8th

1f) Forgiving Family Members When They Hurt You 26
Read On: January 6th | March 23rd | June 8th | August 24th | November 9th

1g) Learning to be a Good Marriage Partner 28
Read On: January 7th | March 24th | June 9th | August 25th | November 10th

Chapter 2
Scripture Therapy To Help Men Conquer
RELATIONSHIP ISSUES 31

2a) Avoiding Harmful Relationships 32
Read On: January 8th | March 25th | June 10th | August 26th | November 11th

2b) Learning to Get Along With Other People 34
Read On: January 9th | March 26th | June 11th | August 27th | November 12th

2c) Conquering Feelings of Loneliness 36
Read On: January 10th | March 27th | June 12th | August 28th | November 13th

2d) Being a Good Friend 38
Read On: January 11th | March 28th | June 13th | August 29th | November 14th

2e) Being Patient and Tolerant With Others 40
Read On: January 12th | March 29th | June 14th | August 30th | November 15th

Chapter 3
Scripture Therapy To Help Men Conquer
EMOTIONAL ISSUES 43

3a) Conquering Fear, Worry, and Anxiety. 44
Read On: January 13th | March 30th | June 15th | August 31st | November 16th

3b) Conquering Sadness and Depression 46
Read On: January 14th | March 31st | June 16th | September 1st | November 17th

3c) Conquering Feelings of Discouragement 48
Read On: January 15th | April 1st | June 17th | September 2nd | November 18th

3d) Faith in God to See You Through Tough Times 50
Read On: January 16th | April 2nd | June 18th | September 3rd | November 19th

3e) Conquering Emotional Stress 52
Read On: January 17th | April 3rd | June 19th | September 4th | November 20th

3f) Encouragement to Conquer Tough Issues 54
Read On: January 18th | April 4th | June 20th | September 5th | November 21st

Chapter 4
Scripture Therapy To Help Men Conquer
ADDICTION ISSUES 57

4a) Conquering The Urge to Give in to Temptation 58
Read On: January 19th | April 5th | June 21st | September 6th | November 22nd

4b) Conquering Addictions and Bad Habits 60
Read On: January 20th | April 6th | June 22nd | September 7th | November 23rd

4c) The Lord's Help Conquering Addictions 62
Read On: January 21st | April 7th | June 23rd | September 8th | November 24th

4d) Conquering Addiction to Pornography 64
Read On: January 22nd | April 8th | June 24th | September 9th | November 25th

4e) Conquering Addiction to Masturbation 66
Read On: January 23rd | April 9th | June 25th | September 10th | November 26th

4f) Conquering Sexual Unfaithfulness 68
Read On: January 24th | April 10th | June 26th | September 11th | November 27th

4g) Conquering Lust and Harmful Sexual Addictions 70
Read On: January 25th | April 11th | June 27th | September 12th | November 28th

4h) Conquering Addiction to Alcohol or Drugs 72
Read On: January 26th | April 12th | June 28th | September 13th | November 29th

Chapter 5
Scripture Therapy To Help Men Conquer FINANCIAL ISSUES 75

5a) Being Faithful to The Lord With Your Finances 76
Read On: January 27th | April 13th | June 29th | September 14th | November 30th

5b) Conquering Selfishness by Being Generous 79
Read On: January 28th | April 14th | June 30th | September 15th | December 1st

5c) Conquering Your Financial Struggles 82
Read On: January 29th | April 15th | July 1st | September 16th | December 2nd

5d) Having Enough Money to Meet Your Needs 84
Read On: January 30th | April 16th | July 2nd | September 17th | December 3rd

5e) Conquering Poverty and Lack 86
Read On: January 31st | April 17th | July 3rd | September 18th | December 4th

Chapter 6
Scripture Therapy To Help Men Conquer HEALTH ISSUES 89

6a) Staying Strong and Healthy 90
Read On: February 1st | April 18th | July 4th | September 19th | December 5th

6b) God's Protection Over Your Life 92
Read On: February 2nd | April 19th | July 5th | September 20th | December 6th

6c) Protection From Harm or Danger 94
Read On: February 3rd | April 20th | July 6th | September 21st | December 7th

6d) Healing From Sickness and Disease 96
Read On: February 4th | April 21st | July 7th | September 22nd | December 8th

6e) Staying Mentally and Emotionally Healthy 99
Read On: February 5th | April 22nd | July 8th | September 23rd | December 9th

6f) The Lord's Protection From Illness and Disease 101
Read On: February 6th | April 23rd | July 9th | September 24th | December 10th

Chapter 7
Scripture Therapy To Help Men Conquer SUCCESS ISSUES 103

7a) Conquering The Fears Limiting Your Potential 104
Read On: February 7th | April 24th | July 10th | September 25th | December 11th

7b) The Lord's Guidance to Help You Succeed 106
Read On: February 8th | April 25th | July 11th | September 26th | December 12th

7c) Conquering Barriers to Your Success 108
Read On: February 9th | April 26th | July 12th | September 27th | December 13th

7d) Determination to Persevere Through Challenges 111
Read On: February 10th | April 27th | July 13th | September 28th | December 14th

7e) Conquering The Challenges You Face in Life 114
Read On: February 11th | April 28th | July 14th | September 29th | December 15th

7f) Belief in God's Covenant Promise to Bless You 117
Read On: February 12th | April 29th | July 15th | September 30th | December 16th

7g) Inspiration to Conquer Your Fears and Doubts 120
Read On: February 13th | April 30th | July 16th | October 1st | December 17th

7h) Your Motivation to Work Hard and Succeed 123
Read On: February 14th | May 1st | July 17th | October 2nd | December 18th

7i) Self-Belief to Succeed in Everything You Do 126
Read On: February 15th | May 2nd | July 18th | October 3rd | December 19th

7j) Confidence in God to Provide for Your Needs 129
Read On: February 16th | May 3rd | July 19th | October 4th | December 20th

7k) Your Confidence and Determination to Succeed 132
Read On: February 17th | May 4th | July 20th | October 5th | December 21st

Chapter 8
Scripture Therapy To Help Men Conquer
PERSONALITY ISSUES 135

8a) Patience in Listening to Other People's Views. 136
Read On: February 18th | May 5th | July 21st | October 6th | December 22nd

8b) Having a Gentle Personality 139
Read On: February 19th | May 6th | July 22nd | October 7th | December 23rd

8c) Removing Bad Habits From Your Personality 142
Read On: February 20th | May 7th | July 23rd | October 8th | December 24th

8d) Developing a Christian Personality. 145
Read On: February 21st | May 8th | July 24th | October 9th | December 25th

8e) Having a Confident Personality 148
Read On: February 22nd | May 9th | July 25th | October 10th | December 26th

8f) Having a Personality That Pleases The Lord 150
Read On: February 23rd | May 10th | July 26th | October 11th | December 27th

Chapter 9
Scripture Therapy To Help Men Conquer
LIFESTYLE ISSUES 153

9a) Living a Christian Lifestyle 154
Read On: February 24th | May 11th | July 27th | October 12th | December 28th

9b) Living a Lifestyle That Pleases The Lord. 156
Read On: February 25th | May 12th | July 28th | October 13th | December 29th

9c) Help Conquering Your Bad Habits. 159
Read On: February 26th | May 13th | July 29th | October 14th | December 30th

9d) Learning to Live a Pure and Holy Lifestyle 161
Read On: February 27th | May 14th | July 30th | October 15th | December 31st

9e) Making Positive Changes to Your Lifestyle 163
Read On: February 28th | May 15th | July 31st | October 16th

Chapter 10
Scripture Therapy To Help Men Conquer
ATTITUDE ISSUES 165

10a) Keeping a Positive Attitude at All Times 166
Read On: February 29th | May 16th | August 1st | October 17th

10b) Showing Kindness and Humility in Your Attitude 169
Read On: March 1st | May 17th | August 2nd | October 18th

10c) Changing Negative Parts of Your Attitude 171
Read On: March 2nd | May 18th | August 3rd | October 19th

10d) Developing a Christ-Like Attitude 173
Read On: March 3rd | May 19th | August 4th | October 20th

10e) Having a Good Attitude towards Life 176
Read On: March 4th | May 20th | August 5th | October 21st

10f) Controlling Your Attitude When Angry 178
Read On: March 5th | May 21st | August 6th | October 22nd

Chapter 11
Scripture Therapy To Help Men Conquer
SPIRITUAL GROWTH ISSUES 181

11a) Confidence in The Power of Your Prayers 182
Read On: March 6th | May 22nd | August 7th | October 23rd

11b) Obeying The Lord With All Your Heart 185
Read On: March 7th | May 23rd | August 8th | October 24th

11c) Being Faithful to Obey God's Commands 187
Read On: March 8th | May 24th | August 9th | October 25th

11d) Getting Sin Out of Your Lifestyle 189
Read On: March 9th | May 25th | August 10th | October 26th

11e) Having Faith and Trust in The Lord .192
Read On: March 10th | May 26th | August 11th | October 27th

11f) Being Faithful to Worship The Lord Daily 195
Read On: March 11th | May 27th | August 12th | October 28th

11g) Victory Over The Power of Your Enemy 197
Read On: March 12th | May 28th | August 13th | October 29th

Chapter 12
Scripture Therapy To Help Men Conquer
LAWFUL BEHAVIOUR ISSUES 201

12a) Abiding by the Law at All Times 202
Read On: March 13th | May 29th | August 14th | October 30th

12b) Living a Life of Obedience to God's Commands 204
Read On: March 14th | May 30th | August 15th | October 31st

12c) Getting Rid of Your Bad Behaviour 207
Read On: March 15th | May 31st | August 16th | November 1st

12d) Being a Law-Abiding Citizen 210
Read On: March 16th | June 1st | August 17th | November 2nd

12e) Getting Rid of a Criminal Lifestyle .213
Read On: March 17th | June 2nd | August 18th | November 3rd

Other Books by Scripture Therapy Resources 217
Testimonies 219

Preface

Life can be a really wonderful experience particularly when all is going well for us and we have little or no worrying problems to have to deal with. But as we all know every now and then we find ourselves faced with difficult and challenging issues which need to be dealt with quickly and effectively otherwise they end up stealing away our joy and happiness.

From my years of experience as a professional counselling therapist I have come across many well meaning people both young and old who struggle with trying to overcome challenging issues in their lives. Having been through a few challenges myself I am no stranger to the stress that comes when faced with overwhelming situations. One of the main reasons why I created the *Scripture Therapy Daily Devotional* series is to provide user-friendly books that apply biblical scripture as a means of self-help therapy for dealing with life's difficult and challenging issues.

Biblical scriptures can help immensely in ones journey through life. The wisdom they contain provides guidance to help overcome many of life's challenges. It should be no secret to any Christian that the source of wisdom and knowledge to overcome any of life's difficult and challenging issues can be found in the Word of God. This is nothing new as it is taught in churches all over the world.

Each title in the Scripture Therapy Daily Devotional series is specifically designed to be user-friendly for its intended audience. The content of each book focuses on helping to change unhealthy thoughts, behaviours and emotions that prevent the enjoyment of a happy, healthy, more fulfilling life. They also serve as a valuable source of wisdom and knowledge to enrich life and support the accomplishment of goals, dreams and desires.

It is my desire and prayer therefore that this devotional does all it was created to do in the life of its reader. May you always find strength and wisdom from the scriptures to overcome any of life's difficult and challenging issues.

God Bless
Benjamin Opaleye

How to Get The Most Out of This Devotional

CELL GROUP / HOME FELLOWSHIP Bible Study Programme

STEP 1: Meet weekly in home cell groups for fellowship, fun, and Bible study.

STEP 2: Select a fresh topic for study and discussion using either the Men, Women, Teen or Success Devotional.

STEP 3: Read out the scriptures in the topic you have chosen to study.

STEP 4: Each person should then highlight in their devotional 3 inspirational and uplifting scriptures and share with the group how the scriptures inspire them. Allow each person 5 minutes to express their thoughts and feelings.

STEP 5: Allow an additional 20-30 minutes for open and interactive discussion. Share testimonies and practical experiences of how scriptures have come alive in your lives or in the lives of others you know of.

STEP 6: The group leader can round up by praying for everyone.

The Men, Women, and Teen Devotional contain identical scriptures and can be used in the same Bible study group.

PERSONAL Bible Study Programme

STEP 1: Dedicate a time to read at least one topic from your devotional daily.

STEP 2: Use the contents page to help guide you in selecting a fresh topic.

STEP 3: Highlight 3 inspirational and uplifting scriptures from each topic and think on those scriptures throughout your day.

STEP 4: Do not deceive yourselves by just listening to his word; instead, put it into practice. – **James 1:22 (GNB)**

COUPLES Bible Study Programme

STEP 1: Dedicate a special time each week to come together as a couple for a few minutes of intimate Bible study.

STEP 2: Take turns in selecting a fresh topic for study and discussion using either the Men, Women, or Success Devotional.

STEP 3: Read through the scriptures in the topic you have chosen to study.

Scripture Therapy Daily Devotional For Men

STEP 4: Highlight in your individual devotionals 3 inspirational and uplifting scriptures and share with each other why you feel inspired by them. Allow 10 minutes each to express your inspired thoughts and feelings.

STEP 5: Allow an additional 20-30 minutes for open and interactive discussion. Share testimonies and practical experiences of how scriptures have come alive in your lives or in the lives of others you know of.

STEP 6: Round up by praying for each other.

FAMILY Bible Study Programme

STEP 1: Dedicate a time each week for family fellowship, fun, and Bible study.

STEP 2: Select a fresh topic for study and discussion using either the Men, Women, Teen or Success Devotional.

STEP 3: Read out the scriptures in the topic you have chosen to study.

STEP 4: Each family member should then highlight in their devotional 3 inspirational and uplifting scriptures and share how the scriptures inspire them. Allow 5 minutes each to express your inspired thoughts and feelings.

STEP 5: Allow an additional 20-30 minutes for open and interactive discussion. Share testimonies and practical experiences of how you have seen scriptures come alive in your lives or in the lives of others you know of.

STEP 6: Round up by praying for members of the family.

The Men, Women, Teen and Children's Devotional contain identical scriptures and can be used in the same Bible study group.

YOUTH GROUP Bible Study Programme

STEP 1: Meet weekly in youth groups for fun, fellowship and Bible study.

STEP 2: Select a fresh topic for study and discussion using either the Men, Women, or Teen Devotional.

STEP 3: Read out the scriptures in the topic you have chosen to study.

STEP 4: Each person should then highlight in their devotional 3 inspirational and uplifting scriptures and share with the group how the scriptures inspire them. Allow each person 5 minutes to express their thoughts and feelings.

STEP 5: Allow an additional 20-30 minutes for open and interactive discussion. Share testimonies and practical experiences of how scriptures have come alive in your lives or in the lives of others you know of.

STEP 6: The group leader can round up by praying for everyone.

For youth aged 20 and above use the Men and Women Devotional in place of the Teen. All 3 devotionals contain identical scriptures and can be used in the same Bible study group.

CHILDREN'S Bible Study Programme

STEP 1: Meet weekly with children for fellowship, fun, and Bible study.
STEP 2: Use the children's devotional to select a topic for study and discussion.
STEP 3: Provide a short explanation of what the topic is all about.
STEP 4: Read or allow the kids to read aloud the scriptures in the chosen topic.
STEP 5: Select 2 or 3 scriptures and use them to tell stories to the children. This can be demonstrated through drama skits and play acting involving the kids.

CHAPTER 1

FAMILY ISSUES

TOPICS

1a) Protection Over You and Your Family Members
Read On: January 1st | March 18th | June 3rd | August 19th | November 4th

1b) Maintaining Peace and Harmony at Home
Read On: January 2nd | March 19th | June 4th | August 20th | November 5th

1c) Keeping A Healthy Parent-Child Relationship
Read On: January 3rd | March 20th | June 5th | August 21st | November 6th

1d) Showing Love to Your Family Members
Read On: January 4th | March 21st | June 6th | August 22nd | November 7th

1e) Controlling Your Temper When Family Upset You
Read On: January 5th | March 22nd | June 7th | August 23rd | November 8th

1f) Forgiving Family Members When They Hurt You
Read On: January 6th | March 23rd | June 8th | August 24th | November 9th

1g) Learning to be a Good Marriage Partner
Read On: January 7th | March 24th | June 9th | August 25th | November 10th

1a) Protection Over You and Your Family Members

Read On: January 1st | March 18th | June 3rd | August 19th | November 4th

1) I lie down and sleep, and all night long **the LORD protects me.** — *Psalm 3:5 GNB*

2) I can lie down and sleep soundly **because you, LORD, will keep me safe.** — *Psalm 4:8 CEV*

3) The LORD is my light and my salvation; I will fear no one. **The LORD protects me from all danger;** I will never be afraid. — *Psalm 27:1 GNB*

4) You hide them in the safety of your presence from the plots of others; in a safe shelter you hide them from the insults of their enemies. — *Psalm 31:20 GNB*

5) The Angel of the Lord encamps around those who fear Him [who revere and worship Him with awe] and each of them He delivers. — *Psalm 34:7 AMP*

6) Live under the protection **of God Most High** and stay in the shadow of God All-Powerful. ²Then you will say to the LORD, "You are my fortress, my place of safety; you are my God, and I trust you." — *Psalm 91:1-2 CEV*

7) He will keep you safe from all **hidden dangers** and from all **deadly diseases.** —*Psalm 91:3 GNB*

8) He will cover you with his wings; **you will be safe in his care;** his faithfulness will **protect** and **defend** you. — *Psalm 91:4 (GNB)*

9) You need not fear any dangers at night or sudden attacks during the day ⁶or the plagues that strike in the dark or the evils that kill in daylight. — *Psalm 91:5-6 GNB*

Scripture Therapy Daily Devotional For Men

10) You will not be harmed, though thousands fall all around you.
— *Psalm 91:7 CEV*

11) You have made the L*ord* your defender, the Most High your protector, ¹⁰and so no disaster will strike you, no violence will come near your home. — *Psalm 91:9-10 GNB*

12) and no terrible disasters will strike you or your home.
— *Psalm 91:10 CEV*

13) God will put his angels in charge of you to protect you wherever you go.
— *Psalm 91:11 GNB*

14) God says, "I will save those who love me and will protect those who acknowledge me as L*ord*.
— *Psalm 91:14 GNB*

15) When you are in trouble, call out to me. I will answer and be there to protect and honour you. — *Psalm 91:15 CEV*

16) You will not be afraid when you go to bed, and you will sleep soundly through the night. — *Proverbs 3:24 GNB*

17) You can be sure that the L*ord* will protect you from harm. — *Proverbs 3:26 CEV*

18) You will guard him and keep him in perfect and constant peace whose mind [both its inclination and its character] is stayed on You, because he commits himself to You, leans on You, and hopes confidently in You. — *Isaiah 26:3 AMP*

19) But not a hair of your head shall perish.
— *Luke 21:18 AMP*

20) "Do not be worried and upset," Jesus told them. "Believe in God and believe also in me.
— *John 14:1 GNB*

21) But the L*ord* can be trusted to make you strong and protect you from harm. — *2 Thessalonians 3:3 CEV*

22) The L*ord* will always keep me from being harmed by evil, and he will bring me safely into his heavenly kingdom. Praise him forever and ever! Amen. — *2 Timothy 4:18 CEV*

1b) Maintaining Peace and Harmony
at Home

Read On: January 2nd | March 19th | June 4th | August 20th | November 5th

1) **Fools who cause trouble in the family won't inherit a thing.** They will end up as slaves of someone with good sense. — *Proverbs 11:29 CEV*

2) It is truly wonderful **when relatives live together in peace.** — *Psalm 133:1 CEV*

3) **Never let go of loyalty and faithfulness.** Tie them round your neck; write them on your heart. — *Proverbs 3:3 GNB*

4) You will have to live with the consequences of everything you say. — *Proverbs 18:20 GNB*

5) **What you say can preserve life or destroy it;** so you must accept the consequences of **your words.** — *Proverbs 18:21 GNB*

6) But He said, **Blessed** (happy and to be envied) rather **are those** who **hear the Word of God** and **obey** and **practice it!** — *Luke 11:28 AMP*

7) A man **should fulfill his duty as a husband,** and a woman **should fulfill her duty as a wife,** and each should **satisfy the other's needs.** — *1 Corinthians 7:3 GNB*

8) Stop being bitter and angry with others. Don't yell at one another or curse each other or ever be rude. — *Ephesians 4:31 CEV*

9) Instead, be kind and tender-hearted to one another, and forgive one another, as God has forgiven you through Christ. — *Ephesians 4:32 GNB*

10) A husband should love his wife as much as Christ loved the church and gave his life for it. — *Ephesians 5:25 CEV*

11) God loves you and has chosen you as his own special people. So be gentle, kind, humble, meek, and patient. — *Colossians 3:12 CEV*

12) Be tolerant with one another and forgive one another whenever any of you has a complaint against someone else. You must forgive one another just as the Lord has forgiven you. — *Colossians 3:13 GNB*

Scripture Therapy Daily Devotional For Men

13) And God's servants **must not be troublemakers**. They must be **kind to everyone,** and they must be **good teachers and very patient.** — *2 Timothy 2:24 CEV*

14) Be humble when you correct people who oppose you. Perhaps God will lead them to turn to him and learn **the truth.** — *2 Timothy 2:25 CEV*

15) Our great desire is that **each of you keep up your eagerness to the end,** so that the things you hope for **will come true.** — *Hebrews 6:11 GNB*

16) We do not want you to become **lazy,** but to be like **those who believe** and are **patient,** and so **receive** what God has **promised.** — *Hebrews 6:12 GNB*

17) Learn to be patient, so that you will **please God** and be given what he has **promised.** — *Hebrews 10:36 CEV*

18) Have respect for marriage. Always be faithful to your partner, because God will punish anyone who is immoral or **unfaithful** in marriage. — *Hebrews 13:4 CEV*

19) Don't grumble about each other or you will be judged, and the judge is just outside the door. — *James 5:9 CEV*

20) If you are a husband, you should be **thoughtful** of your wife. **Treat her with honour,** because she isn't as strong as you are, and **she shares with you in the gift of life.** Then **nothing** will stand **in the way of your prayers.** — *1 Peter 3:7 CEV*

21) Finally, all [of you] should be of one and the same mind (**united** in spirit), **sympathizing** [with one another], loving [each other] as brethren [of one household], **compassionate** and **courteous** (tenderhearted and humble). — *1 Peter 3:8 AMP*

22) Never return evil for evil or insult for insult (scolding, tongue-lashing, berating), but on the contrary **blessing [praying for their welfare, happiness, and protection, and truly pitying and loving them].** For know that to this you have been called, **that you may yourselves inherit a blessing [from God —** that you may obtain a blessing as heirs, bringing welfare and happiness and protection]. — *1 Peter 3:9 AMP*

1c) Keeping a Healthy
Parent-Child Relationship

Read On: January 3rd | March 20th | June 5th | August 21st | November 6th

1) Love the LORD your God, obey him and be faithful to him, and then you and your descendants will live long in the land that he promised to give your ancestors, Abraham, Isaac, and Jacob."
— *Deuteronomy 30:20 GNB*

2) When a wife has no children, he blesses her with some, and she is happy. Shout praises to the LORD!
— *Psalm 113:9 CEV*

3) I will never neglect your instructions, because by them you have kept me alive. — *Psalm 119:93 GNB*

4) Children are a blessing and a gift from the LORD.
— *Psalm 127:3 CEV*

5) My child, listen carefully to everything I say.
— *Proverbs 4:20 CEV*

6) Children with good sense accept correction from their parents, but stubborn children ignore it completely.
— *Proverbs 13:1 CEV*

7) If you love your children, you will correct them; if you don't love them, you won't correct them. — *Proverbs 13:24 CEV*

8) A gentle answer quietens anger, but a harsh one stirs it up.
— *Proverbs 15:1 GNB*

9) If you pay attention when you are corrected, you are wise. — *Proverbs 15:31 GNB*

10) Healthy correction is good, and if you accept it, you will be wise.
— *Proverbs 15:31 CEV*

11) You hurt only yourself by rejecting instruction, but it makes good sense to accept it. — *Proverbs 15:32 CEV*

12) Pay attention to advice and accept correction, so you can live sensibly.
— *Proverbs 19:20 CEV*

13) Teach your children right from wrong, and when they are grown they will still do right.
— *Proverbs 22:6 CEV*

Scripture Therapy Daily Devotional For Men

14) **Patience and gentle talk** can convince a ruler and **overcome any problem.**
— *Proverbs 25:15 CEV*

15) **Don't be cruel to any of these little ones!** I promise you that their angels are always with my Father in heaven.
— *Matthew 18:11 CEV*

16) But Jesus said, **"Let the children come to me, and don't try to stop them!** People who are like these children belong to God's kingdom." — *Matthew 19:14 CEV*

18) So [instead of **further rebuke,** now] you should rather turn and **[graciously] forgive and comfort** *and* **encourage [him],** to keep him from being overwhelmed by excessive sorrow and despair.
— *2 Corinthians 2:7 AMP*

17) God is the one who makes us patient and cheerful. **I pray that he will help you live at peace with each other,** as you follow Christ. — *Romans 15:5 CEV*

19) Instead, **by speaking the truth in a spirit of love,** we must **grow up** in every way to Christ, who is the head.
— *Ephesians 4:15 GNB*

20) Children, it is your Christian duty to obey your parents, for this is the **right thing to do.** ²**"Respect your father and mother"** is the first commandment **that has a promise added:** ³**"so that all may go well with you,** and you may live a long time in the land." — *Ephesians 6:1-3 GNB*

21) **Parents, do not treat your children in such a way as to make them angry.** Instead, bring them up with **Christian discipline and instruction.** — *Ephesians 6:4 GNB*

22) Fathers, do not provoke *or* **irritate** *or* **fret your children** [do not be hard on them or harass them], **lest they become discouraged** and **sullen** and **morose** and **feel inferior and frustrated.** **[Do not break their spirit.]**— *Colossians 3:21 AMP*

23) **There is no fear in love; perfect love drives out all fear.** So then, love has not been made perfect in **anyone who is afraid,** because fear has to do with punishment. — *1 John 4:18 GNB*

24) **Nothing brings me greater happiness than to hear that my children are obeying the truth.** — *3 John 1:4 CEV*

1d) Showing Love to
Your Family Members

Read On: January 4th | March 21st | June 6th | August 22nd | November 7th

1) How wonderful it is, how pleasant, **for God's people to live together in harmony!** — *Psalm 133:1 GNB*

2) **What matters most is loyalty.** It's better to be poor than to be a liar. — *Proverbs 19:22 CEV*

3) Through skillful *and* **godly Wisdom is a house (a life, a home, a family) built,** and by understanding it is established [on a sound and good foundation]. — *Proverbs 24:3 AMP*

4) You have heard people say, **"Love your neighbours** and hate your enemies." 44**But I tell you to love your enemies and pray for anyone who ill-treats you.** — *Matthew 5:43-44 CEV*

5) "And I tell you more: whenever two of you on earth agree about anything you pray for, it will be done for you by my Father in heaven. — *Matthew 18:19 GNB*

6) **Whenever two or three of you come together in my name, I am there with you.** — *Matthew 18:20 CEV*

7) By this **shall all [men] know** that you are My disciples, **if you love one another** [if you keep on showing love among yourselves]. — *John 13:35 AMP*

8) They replied, **"Have faith in the Lord Jesus** and you will be saved! This is also true **for everyone who lives in your home."** — *Acts 16:31 CEV*

9) **Love each other as brothers and sisters** and honour others more than you do yourself. — *Romans 12:10 CEV*

10) My dear friends, as a **follower** of our Lord Jesus Christ, **I beg you to get along with each other.** Don't take sides. Always **try to agree** in what you think. — *1 Corinthians 1:10 CEV*

Scripture Therapy Daily Devotional For Men

11) I may be able to speak the languages of human beings and even of angels, **but if I have no love,** my speech is no more than a noisy gong or a clanging bell. *—1 Corinthians 13:1 GNB*

12) Always be **humble** and **gentle. Patiently put up with each other** and **love each other.** *— Ephesians 4:2 CEV*

13) Do your best to preserve the unity which the Spirit gives by means of the peace that binds you together. *— Ephesians 4:3 GNB*

14) Do not use harmful words, but only **helpful words,** the kind that build up and provide what is **needed,** so that **what you say will do good** to those who hear you. *— Ephesians 4:29 GNB*

15) I pray that your love will keep on growing more and more, together with true knowledge and perfect judgment. *— Philippians 1:9 GNB*

16) But now you must stop doing such things. **You must stop being angry, hateful, and evil. You must no longer say insulting or cruel things about others.** *— Colossians 3:8 CEV*

17) Love is more important than anything else. It is what ties everything completely together. *— Colossians 3:14 CEV*

18) Let us be concerned for one another, to **help** one another to **show love and to do good.** *— Hebrews 10:24 GNB*

19) My dear friends, you should be **quick to listen** and **slow to speak or to get angry.** *— James 1:19 CEV*

20) Finally, all [of you] should be of one *and* the same mind (united in spirit), sympathizing [with one another], loving [each other] as brethren [of one household], compassionate and courteous (tenderhearted and humble). *— 1 Peter 3:8 AMP*

21) Don't be hateful and insult people just because they are hateful and insult you. Instead, treat everyone **with kindness.** You are God's chosen ones, **and he will bless you.** The Scriptures say. *— 1 Peter 3:9 CEV*

1e) Controlling Your Temper
When Family Upset You

Read On: January 5th | March 22nd | June 7th | August 23rd | November 8th

1) **Be careful** how you think; your **life** is **shaped** by your **thoughts.**
— *Proverbs 4:23 GNB*

2) **Fools have quick tempers,** and no one likes you if you can't be trusted.
— *Proverbs 14:17 CEV*

3) If you stay calm, you are wise, but if you have a **hot temper,** you only show how **stupid you are.** — *Proverbs 14:29 GNB*

4) It's clever to be patient, but **it's stupid to lose your temper.** — *Proverbs 14:29 CEV*

5) When people are **happy, they smile,** but when they are **sad, they look depressed.**
— *Proverbs 15:13 GNB*

6) **Losing your temper causes a lot of trouble,** but staying **calm** settles arguments.
— *Proverbs 15:18 CEV*

7) What a **joy** it is to find **just the right word** for the **right occasion!** — *Proverbs 15:23 GNB*

8) **Kind words** are like honey — they **cheer you up** and **make you feel strong.**
— *Proverbs 16:24 CEV*

9) It is better to be patient than **powerful.** It is better to **win control over yourself** than over whole cities. — *Proverbs 16:32 GNB*

10) Without wood, a fire goes out; without gossip, quarrelling stops.
— *Proverbs 26:20 GNB*

11) Don't be a fool and quickly lose your temper — be sensible and patient. — *Proverbs 29:11 CEV*

12) A person with a quick temper stirs up **arguments** and commits a lot of sins. — *Proverbs 29:22 CEV*

13) Better is the end of a thing than the beginning of it, and **the patient in spirit** is better than **the proud in spirit.** — *Ecclesiastes 7:8 AMP*

Scripture Therapy Daily Devotional For Men

14) Only fools **get angry quickly** and **hold a grudge.** — *Ecclesiastes 7:9 CEV*

15) And said, Truly I say to you, **unless you repent (change, turn about) and become like little children [trusting, lowly, loving, forgiving],** you can never enter the kingdom of heaven [at all]. — *Matthew 18:3 AMP*

16) This is My commandment: **that you love one another** [just] **as I have loved you.** — *John 15:12 AMP*

17) God is the one who makes us patient and cheerful. **I pray that he will help you live at peace with each other,** as you follow Christ. — *Romans 15:5 CEV*

18) Stop being bitter and angry with others. Don't yell at one another or curse each other or ever be rude. — *Ephesians 4:31 CEV*

19) Now, the important thing is that your way of life should be as the gospel of Christ requires, so that, whether or not I am able to go and see you, I will hear that you are standing firm with one common purpose and that with only one desire you are fighting together for the faith of the gospel. — *Philippians 1:27 GNB*

20) Remind your people of this, and give them a **solemn warning** in God's presence **not to fight over words.** It does no good, **but only ruins the people who listen.** — *2 Timothy 2:14 GNB*

21) Make sure that no one misses out on God's wonderful kindness. **Don't let anyone become bitter and cause trouble for the rest of you.** — *Hebrews 12:15 CEV*

22) If you are angry, **you cannot do any of the good things that God wants done.** — *James 1:20 CEV*

23) Finally, all of you should agree and **have concern and love for each other.** You should also be **kind and humble.** — *1 Peter 3:8 CEV*

1f) Forgiving Family Members
When They Hurt You

Read On: January 6th | March 23rd | June 8th | August 24th | November 9th

1) Teach me, LORD, what you want me to do, and I will obey you faithfully; teach me to serve you with complete devotion. — *Psalm 86:11 GNB*

2) But I tell you to love your enemies and pray for anyone who ill-treats you. — *Matthew 5:44 CEV*

3) "If you forgive others the wrongs they have done to you, your Father in heaven will also forgive you. [15]But if you do not forgive others, then your Father will not forgive the wrongs you have done. — *Matthew 6:14-15 GNB*

4) But I am giving you a new command. You must love each other, just as I have loved you. — *John 13:34 CEV*

5) Bless those who persecute you [who are cruel in their attitude toward you]; bless and do not curse them. — *Romans 12:14 AMP*

6) love is not ill-mannered or selfish or irritable; love does not keep a record of wrongs. — *1 Corinthians 13:5 GNB*

7) May Christ through your faith [actually] dwell (settle down, abide, make His permanent home) in your hearts! May you be rooted deep in love *and* founded securely on love. — *Ephesians 3:17 AMP*

8) Don't get so angry that you sin. Don't go to bed angry. — *Ephesians 4:26 CEV*

9) Since you are God's dear children, you must try to be like him. - *Ephesians 5:1 GNB*

10) So be careful how you live. Don't live like ignorant people, but like wise people. — *Ephesians 5:15 GNB*

Scripture Therapy Daily Devotional For Men

11) And look out for one another's interests, not just for your own. — *Philippians 2:4 GNB*

12) The attitude you should have is the one that Christ Jesus had. — *Philippians 2:5 GNB*

13) Brethren, together follow my example and observe those who live after the pattern we have set for you. — *Philippians 3:17 AMP*

14) God loves you and has chosen you as his own special people. So be gentle, kind, humble, meek, and patient. — *Colossians 3:12 CEV*

15) Put up with each other, and forgive anyone who does you wrong, just as Christ has forgiven you. — *Colossians 3:13 CEV*

16) Why do you fight and argue with each other? Isn't it because you are full of selfish desires that fight to control your body? — *James 4:1 CEV*

17) We truly love God only when we obey him as we should, and then we know that we belong to him. — *1 John 2:5 CEV*

18) My children, our love should not be just words and talk; it must be true love, which shows itself in action. — *1 John 3:18 GNB*

19) God wants us to have faith in his Son Jesus Christ and to love each other. This is also what Jesus taught us to do. — *1 John 3:23 CEV*

20) My dear friends, we must love each other. Love comes from God, and when we love each other, it shows that we have been given new life. We are now God's children, and we know him. — *1 John 4:7 CEV*

21) Dear friends, since God loved us this much, we must love each other. — *1 John 4:11 CEV*

1g) Learning To Be A Good Marriage Partner

Read On: January 7th | March 24th | June 9th | August 25th | November 10th

1) **Never let go of loyalty and faithfulness.** Tie them around your neck; write **them on your heart.**
— *Proverbs 3:3 GNB*

2) **Be faithful to your own wife and give your love to her alone.** 16Children that you have by other women will do you no good.
—*Proverbs 5:15-16 GNB*

3) **So be happy with your wife** and **find your joy** with the woman you married. — *Proverbs 5:18 GNB*

4) Two are better off than one, **because together they can work more effectively.** — *Ecclesiastes 4:9 GNB*

5) Jesus said: **Don't judge others,** and **God won't judge you.** Don't be **hard on others,** and **God won't be hard on you. Forgive** others, and **God will forgive you.** — *Luke 6:37 CEV*

6) **If you give to others, you will be given a full amount in return.** It will be packed down, shaken together, and spilling over into your lap. **The way you treat others is the way you will be treated.**
— *Luke 6:38 CEV*

7) **If you love each other,** everyone will know that you are my disciples.
— *John 13:35 CEV*

8) **No one who loves others will harm them.** So love is all that the Law demands. — *Romans 13:10 CEV*

9) But because of the temptation to impurity *and* to avoid immorality, let each [man] **have his own wife** and let each [woman] **have her own husband.**
— *1 Corinthians 7:2 AMP*

10) Love is always **supportive, loyal, hopeful, and trusting.** — *1 Corinthians 13:7 CEV*

11) **Be always humble, gentle, and patient.** Show your love **by being tolerant** with one another.
—*Ephesians 4:2 GNB*

12) Try your best to let God's Spirit keep your hearts united. Do this by living at peace. — *Ephesians 4:3 CEV*

13) Do not use harmful words, but only **helpful words,** the kind that **build up** and provide what is needed, so that what you say **will do good** to those **who hear you.** — *Ephesians 4:29 GNB*

14) Stop being bitter and **angry with others.** Don't **yell** at one another or **curse** each other or ever be **rude.** — *Ephesians 4:31 CEV*

15) Instead, **be kind and tenderhearted to one another,** and **forgive one another,** as God has forgiven **you** through Christ. — *Ephesians 4:32 GNB*

16) In the same way, **a husband should love his wife as much as he loves himself.** A husband who loves his wife shows that **he loves himself.** — *Ephesians 5:28 CEV*

17) I pray that your love will keep on growing more and more, together with true knowledge and perfect judgment. — *Philippians 1:9 GNB*

18) In conclusion, my brothers and sisters, **fill your minds with those things that are good** and that **deserve praise:** things that are **true, noble, right, pure, lovely,** and **honourable.** — *Philippians 4:8 GNB*

19) A husband **must love** his wife and not **abuse her.** — *Colossians 3:19 CEV*

20) Respect and **honour** your wife. — *1 Thessalonians 4:4 CEV*

21) Let us be concerned for one another, to **help one another** to show **love** and to do **good.** — *Hebrews 10:24 GNB*

22) Finally, **all of you should agree** and **have concern** and **love for each other.** You should also **be kind** and **humble.** — *1 Peter 3:8 CEV*

23) Never return evil for evil or insult for insult (scolding, tongue-lashing, berating), but on the contrary **blessing** [praying for their welfare, happiness, and protection, and truly pitying and loving them]. For *know that* **to this you have been called,** that you may **yourselves inherit a blessing** [from God — that you may obtain a blessing as heirs, bringing welfare and happiness and protection]. — *1 Peter 3:9 AMP*

CHAPTER 2

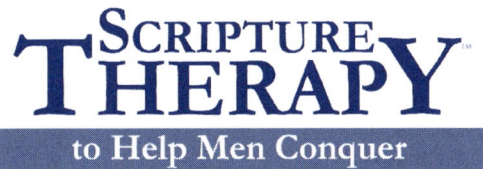

Relationship Issues

TOPICS

2a) Avoiding Harmful Relationships
Read On: January 8th | March 25th | June 10th | August 26th | November 11th

2b) Learning to Get Along With Other People
Read On: January 9th | March 26th | June 11th | August 27th | November 12th

2c) Conquering Feelings of Loneliness
Read On: January 10th | March 27th | June 12th | August 28th | November 13th

2d) Being a Good Friend
Read On: January 11th | March 28th | June 13th | August 29th | November 14th

2e) Being Patient and Tolerant With Others
Read On: January 12th | March 29th | June 14th | August 30th | November 15th

2a) Avoiding
Harmful Relationships

Read On: January 8th | March 25th | June 10th | August 26th | November 11th

1) But the LORD said to him, **"Pay no attention to how tall and handsome he is.** I have rejected him, because I do not judge as people judge. **They look at the outward appearance, but I look at the heart."**
— *1 Samuel 16:7 GNB*

2) Your **insight** and **understanding** will **protect** you [12]**and prevent you from doing the wrong thing.** They will keep you **away** from **people who stir up trouble** by what they say. — *Proverbs 2:11-12 GNB*

3) Children with good sense accept correction from their parents, but stubborn children ignore it completely. — *Proverbs 13:1 CEV*

4) Keep company with the **wise** and you will become wise. If you **make friends with stupid people, you will be ruined.**
—*Proverbs 13:20 GNB*

5) A friend is always a friend, and relatives are born to share our troubles. — *Proverbs 17:17 CEV*

6) Those who are sure of themselves **do not talk all the time. People who stay calm** have real insight.
— *Proverbs 17:27 GNB*

7) Some friends don't help, but a true friend is closer than your own family.
— *Proverbs 18:24 CEV*

8) Just as iron sharpens iron, **friends sharpen the minds of each other.**
— *Proverbs 27:17 CEV*

9) A **young man** who obeys the law is **intelligent.** One who **makes friends with good-for-nothings** is a **disgrace** to his father. — *Proverbs 28:7 GNB*

Scripture Therapy Daily Devotional For Men

10) **It is dangerous to be concerned with what others think of you,** but if you trust the LORD, you are safe. — *Proverbs 29:25 GNB*

11) **You are better off having a friend than being all alone,** because then you will get more enjoyment out of what you earn. —*Ecclesiastes 4:9 CEV*

12) **Keep watch and pray that you will not fall into temptation.** The spirit is willing, but the flesh is weak." — *Matthew 26:41 GNB*

13) **Everyone must obey the state authorities,** because no authority **exists** without **God's permission,** and the existing authorities **have been put there by God.** — *Romans 13:1 GNB*

14) **Whoever opposes the existing authority opposes what God has ordered;** and anyone who does so will bring **judgment on himself.** — *Romans 13:2 GNB*

15) **So behave properly,** as people do in the day. **Don't go to wild parties or get drunk or be vulgar** or **indecent.** Don't **quarrel** or be **jealous.** — *Romans 13:13 CEV*

16) **Don't fool yourselves. Bad friends will destroy you.** —*1 Corinthians 15:33 CEV*

17) **Abstain from evil** [shrink from it and keep aloof from it] in whatever form *or* **whatever kind it may be.** — *1 Thessalonians 5:22 AMP*

18) Let us be **concerned** for one another, **to help one another** to show **love** and to do **good.** — *Hebrews 10:24 GNB*

19) **Be firm in your faith and resist him,** because you know that **your fellow-believers in all the world are going through the same kind of sufferings.** —*1 Peter 5:9 GNB*

33

2b) Learning to Get Along With
Other People

Read On: January 9th | March 26th | June 11th | August 27th | November 12th

1) I won't ever forget your teachings, because you give me new life by following them. — *Psalm 119:93 CEV*

2) Behold, how **good** and how **pleasant** it is **for brethren to dwell together in unity!** — *Psalm 133:1 AMP*

3) Don't try to get even. Trust the LORD, and he will help you. — *Proverbs 20:22 CEV*

4) But I tell you to love your enemies and pray for anyone who ill-treats you. — *Matthew 5:44 CEV*

5) Treat others **just as you want to be treated.** — *Luke 6:31 CEV*

6) So be **merciful** (sympathetic, tender, responsive, and **compassionate**) even as your Father is [all these]. — *Luke 6:36 AMP*

7) I give you a new commandment: **that you should love one another.** Just as I have loved you, **so you too should love one another.** — *John 13:34 AMP*

8) Bless those who persecute you [who are cruel in their attitude toward you]; bless and **do not curse them.** — *Romans 12:14 AMP*

9) All the believers continued together in close fellowship and shared their belongings with one another. — *Acts 2:44 GNB*

10) Let each one of us make it a practice to please (make happy) his neighbor for his good *and* for his true welfare, to edify him [to strengthen him and build him up spiritually] — *Romans 15:2 AMP*

11) We should think about others and not about ourselves. — *1 Corinthians 10:24 CEV*

12) May Christ through your faith [actually] dwell (settle down, abide, make His permanent home) in your hearts! May you be rooted deep in love and founded securely on love. — *Ephesians 3:17*

Scripture Therapy Daily Devotional For Men

13) His intention was the **perfecting** *and* the full equipping of the saints (His consecrated people), [that they should do] the work of ministering toward building up Christ's body (the church). — *Ephesians 4:12 AMP*

14) And **become useful** *and* **helpful** *and* **kind to one another, tenderhearted** (compassionate, understanding, loving-hearted), **forgiving one another** [readily and freely], as God in Christ **forgave you.** — *Ephesians 4:32 AMP*

15) Do as God does. After all, you are his dear children. — *Ephesians 5:1 CEV*

16) Let love be your guide. Christ loved us and offered his life for us as a sacrifice that pleases God. — *Ephesians 5:2 CEV*

17) And look out for one another's interests, not just for your own. — *Philippians 2:4 GNB*

18) Show a gentle attitude towards everyone. The Lord is coming soon. — *Philippians 4:5 GNB*

19) And so encourage one another and help one another, just as you are now doing. — *1 Thessalonians 5:11 GNB*

20) That's also how it is with people. The ones who stop doing evil and make themselves pure will become special. Their lives will be holy and pleasing to their Master, and they will be able to do all kinds of good deeds. — *2 Timothy 2:21 CEV*

21) We should keep on encouraging each other to be thoughtful and to do helpful things. — *Hebrews 10:24 CEV*

22) My brothers and sisters, as believers in our Lord Jesus Christ, the Lord of glory, you must never treat people in different ways according to their outward appearance. — *James 2:1 GNB*

23) Give a kind and respectful answer and keep your conscience clear. This way you will make people ashamed for saying bad things about your good conduct as a follower of Christ. — *1 Peter 3:16 CEV*

24) But as for you, **Christ has poured out his Spirit on you.** As long as his Spirit **remains in you,** you do not need anyone to teach you. For his Spirit **teaches you about everything,** and what he teaches is true, not false. **Obey the Spirit's teaching, then,** and **remain in union with Christ.** — *1 John 2:27 GNB*

2c) Conquering Feelings Of
Loneliness

Read On: January 10th | March 27th | June 12th | August 28th | November 13th

1) The Lord is my Shepherd [to feed, guide, and shield me], I shall not lack. — *Psalm 23:1 AMP*

2) in you, my God, I trust. Save me from the shame of defeat; don't let my enemies gloat over me! — *Psalm 25:2 GNB*

3) Don't give in to worry or anger; it only leads to trouble. — *Psalm 37:8 GNB*

4) You will do everything you have promised; LORD, your love is eternal. Complete the work that you have begun. — *Psalm 138:8 GNB*

5) A simple meal with love is better than a feast where there is hatred. — *Proverbs 15:17 CEV*

6) You will keep your friends if you forgive them, but you will lose your friends if you keep talking about what they did wrong. — *Proverbs 17:9 CEV*

7) It's selfish and stupid to think only of yourself and to sneer at people who have sense. — *Proverbs 18:1 CEV*

8) Some friendships do not last, but some friends are more loyal than brothers. — *Proverbs 18:24 GNB*

9) It is dangerous to be concerned with what others think of you, but if you trust the LORD, you are safe. — *Proverbs 29:25 GNB*

10) Do not be afraid — I am with you! I am your God — let nothing terrify you! I will make you strong and help you; I will protect you and save you. — *Isaiah 41:10 GNB*

11) I will bless you with a future filled with hope — a future of success, not of suffering. — *Jeremiah 29:11 CEV*

12) Jesus said to his disciples, "Don't be worried! Have faith in God and have faith in me. — *John 14:1 CEV*

13) *I give you peace,* **the kind of peace that only I can give.** It isn't like the peace that this world can give. **So don't be worried or afraid.** — *John 14:27 CEV*

14) Jesus told his disciples a story about how they should **keep on praying and never give up.** — *Luke 18:1 CEV*

15) Let your faith be **like a shield,** and you will be able to **stop** all the flaming arrows of the evil one. — *Ephesians 6:16 CEV*

16) Don't worry about anything, **but pray about everything.** With thankful hearts **offer up your prayers and requests to God.** — *Philippians 4:6 CEV*

17) Whatever happens, **keep thanking God because of Jesus Christ.** This is what God wants you to do. — *1 Thessalonians 5:18 CEV*

18) Be glad about this, even though it may now be necessary for you to be sad for a while **because of the many kinds of trials you suffer. ⁷Their purpose is to prove that your faith is genuine.** Even gold, which can be destroyed, is tested by fire; and so **your faith,** which is much more precious than gold, **must also be tested,** so that **it may endure.** Then **you will receive praise** and **glory** and **honour** on the Day when Jesus Christ is revealed. — *1 Peter 1:6-7 GNB*

19) The Lord watches over everyone who obeys him, and he **listens to their prayers.** But he opposes everyone who does evil." — *1 Peter 3:12 CEV*

20) You are better off **to obey God** and suffer **for doing right** than to suffer **for doing wrong.** — *1 Peter 3:17 CEV*

2d) Being a Good Friend

Read On: January 11th | March 28th | June 13th | August 29th | November 14th

1) Don't tell your neighbour to come back tomorrow, **if you can help today.** — *Proverbs 3:28 CEV*

2) Don't try to be mean to **neighbours** who trust you. — *Proverbs 3:29 CEV*

3) Try hard to do right, and you will win friends; go looking for trouble, and you will find it. — *Proverbs 11:27 CEV*

4) It's clever to be patient, but it's stupid **to lose** your **temper.** — *Proverbs 14:29 CEV*

5) Losing your temper causes a lot of trouble, but staying calm settles arguments. — *Proverbs 15:18 CEV*

7) Making up with a friend you have offended is harder than breaking through a city wall. — *Proverbs 18:19 CEV*

6) If you **pay attention when you are corrected,** you are wise. — *Proverbs 15:31 GNB*

8) You will have to **live** with the **consequences** of **everything you say.** — *Proverbs 18:20 GNB*

9) What you say can preserve life or **destroy it;** so you must accept the **consequences** of your words. — *Proverbs 18:21 GNB*

10) Don't desert an old friend of your family or visit your relatives when you are in trouble. **A friend nearby is better than relatives far away.** — *Proverbs 27:10 CEV*

11) I promise you that on the day of judgment, **everyone will have to account for every careless word they have spoken.** — *Matthew 12:36 CEV*

12) If you give to others, you will be given a full amount in return. It will be packed down, shaken together, and spilling over into your lap. **The way you treat others is the way you will be treated.** — *Luke 6:38 CEV*

13) **If you forgive people's sins, they are forgiven;** if you do not forgive them, they are not forgiven." — *John 20:23 GNB*

14) **And put on the new nature** (the regenerate self) created in God's image, **[Godlike]** in true righteousness and holiness. — *Ephesians 4:24 AMP*

15) **Do not use harmful words, but only helpful words,** the kind that **build up** and provide what is needed, so that what you say will do good to those who hear you. — *Ephesians 4:29 GNB*

16) Do everything **without complaining** or **arguing.** —*Philippians 2:14 GNB*

17) Show a gentle attitude towards everyone. The Lord is coming soon. — *Philippians 4:5 GNB*

18) **Whatever you do, work at it with all your heart, as though you were working for the Lord and not for human beings.** ²⁴Remember that the Lord will give you as a reward what he has kept for his people. **For Christ is the real Master you serve.** — *Colossians 3:23-24 GNB*

19) Your speech should always be pleasant and interesting, and you should know how to give **the right answer to everyone.** — *Colossians 4:6 GNB*

20) Remind your people of this, and give them a solemn warning in God's presence **not to fight over words. It does no good,** but only ruins the **people** who **listen.** — *2 Timothy 2:14 GNB*

21) Try to be at peace with everyone, and try to **live a holy life,** because no one will see the Lord without it. — *Hebrews 12:14 GNB*

2e) Being Patient and
Tolerant With Others

Read On: January 12th | March 29th | June 14th | August 30th | November 15th

1) Stop being angry and don't try to take revenge. I am the LORD, and I command you to love others as much as you love yourself. — *Leviticus 19:18 CEV*

2) Behold, how **good** and how **pleasant** it is for brethren to **dwell together in unity!** — *Psalm 133:1 AMP*

3) Kind words are like honey — they cheer you up and make you feel strong. — *Proverbs 16:24 CEV*

4) But I tell you to **love your enemies** and pray for anyone who ill-treats you. — *Matthew 5:44 CEV*

5) This is My commandment: that you love one another [just] as I have loved you. — *John 15:12 AMP*

6) God is the one who makes us patient and cheerful. I pray that he will help you live at peace with each other, as you follow Christ. — *Romans 15:5 CEV*

7) What if I could speak all languages of humans and of angels? **If I did not love others, I would be nothing** more than a noisy gong or a clanging cymbal. — *1 Corinthians 13:1 CEV*

8) Show love in everything you do. — *1 Corinthians 16:14 CEV*

9) I urge you, then — I who am a prisoner because I serve the Lord: **live a life that measures up to the standard God set when he called you.** ²Be always **humble, gentle,** and **patient.** Show your love **by being tolerant with one another.** — *Ephesians 4:1-2 GNB*

10) Stop being bitter and angry with others. Don't **yell at one another** or curse each other or ever be rude. — *Ephesians 4:31 CEV*

11) Instead, **be kind** and **merciful,** and **forgive others,** just as God forgave you because of Christ. — *Ephesians 4:32 CEV*

12) Since you are God's dear children, **you must try to be like him.** — *Ephesians 5:1 GNB*

Scripture Therapy Daily Devotional For Men

13) *Your life must be controlled by love, just as Christ loved us and gave his life for us* as a sweet-smelling offering and sacrifice that pleases God. — *Ephesians 5:2 GNB*

14) Clothe yourselves therefore, as **God's own chosen ones (His own picked representatives),** [who are] **purified** *and* **holy** and well-beloved **[by God Himself, by putting on behavior marked by]** tenderhearted pity and mercy, **kind feeling,** a lowly opinion of yourselves, **gentle ways,** [and] **patience** [which is tireless and long-suffering, and has the power to endure whatever comes, with good temper]. — *Colossians 3:12 AMP*

15) Be tolerant with one another and forgive one another whenever any of you has a complaint against someone else. You must forgive one another just as the Lord has forgiven you. — *Colossians 3:13 GNB*

16) We should keep on encouraging each other to be thoughtful and to do helpful things. — *Hebrews 10:24 CEV*

17) Be beautiful in your heart by being gentle and quiet. This kind of beauty will last, and God considers it very special. — *1 Peter 3:4 CEV*

18) Finally, all of you should agree and have concern and love for each other. You should also be kind and humble. — *1 Peter 3:8 CEV*

19) For this very reason do your best to add goodness to your faith; to your goodness add knowledge; ⁶to your knowledge add self-control; to your self-control add endurance; to your endurance add godliness; ⁷to your godliness add Christian affection; and to your Christian affection add love. — *2 Peter 1:5-7 GNB*

20) These are the qualities you need, and if you have them in abundance, they will make you active and effective in your knowledge of our Lord Jesus Christ. — *2 Peter 1:8 GNB*

21) My children, our love should not be just words and talk; it must be true love, which shows itself in action. — *1 John 3:18 GNB*

CHAPTER 3

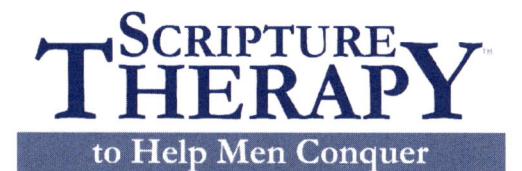

SCRIPTURE THERAPY™ to Help Men Conquer Emotional Issues

TOPICS

3a) Conquering Fear, Worry, and Anxiety
Read On: January 13th | March 30th | June 15th | August 31st | November 16th

3b) Conquering Sadness and Depression
Read On: January 14th | March 31st | June 16th | September 1st | November 17th

3c) Conquering Feelings of Discouragement
Read On: January 15th | April 1st | June 17th | September 2nd | November 18th

3d) Faith in God to See You Through Tough Times
Read On: January 16th | April 2nd | June 18th | September 3rd | November 19th

3e) Conquering Emotional Stress
Read On: January 17th | April 3rd | June 19th | September 4th | November 20th

3f) Encouragement to Conquer Tough Issues
Read On: January 18th | April 4th | June 20th | September 5th | November 21st

3a) Conquering
Fear, Worry, and Anxiety

Read On: January 13th | March 30th | June 15th | August 31st | November 16th

1) The LORD will lead you into the land. **He will always be with you and help you,** so don't ever **be afraid** of your enemies. — *Deuteronomy 31:8 CEV*

2) and Joshua continued, **"Don't ever be afraid or discouraged. Be brave and strong.** This is what the LORD will do to all your enemies." — *Joshua 10:25 CEV*

3) I prayed to the LORD, and he answered me; **he freed me from all my fears.** — *Psalm 34:4 GNB*

4) Let the LORD lead you and trust him to help. — *Psalm 37:5 CEV*

5) Leave your troubles with the LORD, and he will defend you; he never lets honest people be defeated. — *Psalm 55:22 GNB*

6) Do not be afraid — I am with you! I am your God — **let nothing terrify you!** I will make you strong and help you; **I will protect you and save you.** — *Isaiah 41:10 GNB*

7) I promise **to be with you** and **keep you safe, so don't be afraid."** — *Jeremiah 1:8 CEV*

8) "This is why I tell you **not to be worried about the food and drink you need in order to stay alive,** or about clothes for your body. After all, isn't life worth more than food? And isn't the body worth more than clothes? — *Matthew 6:25 GNB*

9) Look at the birds in the sky! They don't plant or harvest. They don't even store grain in barns. **Yet your Father in heaven takes care of them. Aren't you worth more than birds?** — *Matthew 6:26 CEV*

10) Can **worry** make you live longer? — *Matthew 6:27 CEV*

11) "**And why worry about clothes?** Look how the wild flowers grow: they do not work or make clothes for themselves. — *Matthew 6:28 GNB*

12) God gives such beauty to everything that grows in the fields, even though it is here today and thrown into a fire tomorrow. **He will surely do even more for you! Why do you have such little faith?** — *Matthew 6:30 CEV*

13) Only people who don't know God **are always worrying about such things.** Your Father in heaven **knows that you need all of these.** — *Matthew 6:32 CEV*

14) But more than anything else, **put God's work first and do what he wants.** Then the **other things** will be yours as well. — *Matthew 6:33 CEV*

15) Don't worry about tomorrow. It will take care of itself. You have enough to worry about today. — *Matthew 6:34 CEV*

16) And Jesus, replying, said to them, **Have faith in God [constantly].** — *Mark 11:22 AMP*

17) "**Do not be worried and upset,**" Jesus told them. "**Believe in God and believe also in me.** — *John 14:1 GNB*

18) Don't worry about anything, but pray about everything. With thankful hearts **offer up your prayers and requests to God.** — *Philippians 4:6 CEV*

19) In conclusion, my brothers and sisters, **fill your minds with those things that are good and that deserve praise:** things that are true, noble, right, pure, lovely, and honourable. — *Philippians 4:8 GNB*

20) God cares for you, **so turn all your worries over to him.** — *1 Peter 5:7 CEV*

3b) Conquering
Sadness and Depression

Read On: January 14th | March 31st | June 16th | September 1st | November 17th

1) Remember that **I have commanded you to be determined and confident! Don't be afraid or discouraged,** for I, the LORD your God, **am with you wherever you go."** — *Joshua 1:9 GNB*

2) "Go in peace," Eli said, "and may the **God of Israel give you what you have asked him for."** — *1 Samuel 1:17 GNB*

3) Be brave and confident! There's no reason to be afraid of King Sennacherib and his powerful army. **We are much more powerful,** ⁸**because the Lord our God fights on our side.** The Assyrians must rely on human power alone. These words encouraged the army of Judah. — *2 Chronicles 32:7-8 CEV*

4) The LORD is a refuge for the oppressed, **a place of safety in times of trouble.** — *Psalm 9:9 GNB*

5) I was afraid and thought that he had driven me out of his presence. **But he heard my cry, when I called to him for help.** — *Psalm 31:22 GNB*

6) Be strong, be courageous, all you that hope in the LORD. — *Psalm 31:24 GNB*

7) I will always praise the Lord. ²**With all my heart,** I will praise the LORD. Let all who are helpless, listen and be glad. ³Honour the Lord with me! Celebrate his great name. — *Psalm 34:1-3 CEV*

8) Discover for yourself that the Lord is kind. Come to him for protection, and you will be glad. — *Psalm 34:8 CEV*

9) Why am I so sad? Why am I so troubled? I will put my hope in God, and once again I will praise him, my savior and my God. — *Psalm 42:5 GNB*

10) Why am I discouraged? Why am I restless? **I trust you! And I will praise you again** because you help me, and **you are my God.** — *Psalm 43:5 CEV*

Scripture Therapy Daily Devotional For Men

11) but even when **I am afraid, I keep on trusting you.** — *Psalm 56:3 CEV*

12) **I trust in God and am not afraid; I praise him for what he has promised.** What can a mere human being do to me? — *Psalm 56:4 GNB*

13) I am overcome with sorrow. **Encourage me, as you have promised to do.** — *Psalm 119:28 CEV*

14) Being cheerful keeps you healthy. It is slow death to be **gloomy** all the time. — *Proverbs 17:22 GNB*

15) You, Lord, **give perfect peace** to those who keep their purpose firm **and put their trust in you.** — *Isaiah 26:3 GNB*

16) Tell everyone who is discouraged, **"Be strong and don't be afraid! God is coming to your rescue,** coming to punish your enemies." — *Isaiah 35:4 GNB*

18) All of you that honour the LORD and obey the words of his servant, the path you walk may be dark indeed, **but trust in the LORD, rely on your God.** — *Isaiah 50:10 GNB*

17) But those who **trust in the LORD for help will find their strength renewed.** They will rise on wings like eagles; they will run and not get weary; they will walk and **not grow weak.** — *Isaiah 40:31 GNB*

19) I will bless you with a future filled with hope — a future of **success,** not of suffering. — *Jeremiah 29:11 CEV*

20) Then you will call to me. You will come and pray to me, and I will answer you. ¹³You will seek me, and you will find me because you will seek me with all your heart. — *Jeremiah 29:12-13 GNB*

21) I give you peace, the kind of peace that only I can give. It isn't like the peace that this world can give. **So don't be worried or afraid.** —*John 14:27 CEV*

22) God's Spirit doesn't make cowards out of us. **The Spirit gives us power, love, and self-control.** — *2 Timothy 1:7 CEV*

3c) Conquering Feelings of
Discouragement

Read On: January 15th | April 1st | June 17th | September 2nd | November 18th

1) Then Jahaziel said: Your Majesty and everyone from Judah and Jerusalem, **the Lord says that you don't need to be afraid or let this powerful army discourage you. God will fight on your side!** — *2 Chronicles 20:15 CEV*

2) You won't even have to fight. **Just take your positions and watch the Lord rescue you from your enemy.** Don't be afraid. **Just do as you're told.** And as you march out tomorrow, the Lord will be there with you. — *2 Chronicles 20:17 CEV*

3) **I know that I will live to see the LORD'S goodness** in this present life. — *Psalm 27:13 GNB*

4) **Trust in the LORD. Have faith,** do not despair. **Trust** in the LORD. — *Psalm 27:14 GNB*

5) **The LORD is there to rescue all who are discouraged** and have given up hope. — *Psalm 34:18 CEV*

6) **Why am I discouraged?** Why am I restless? **I trust you! And I will praise you again** because you help me, and you are my God. — *Psalm 42:11 CEV*

7) **Hear my prayer, O God;** don't turn away from my plea! — *Psalm 55:1 GNB*

8) **Listen to me and answer me;** I am worn out by my worries. — *Psalm 55:2 GNB*

9) As for me, **I will call upon God,** and the Lord will save me. — *Psalm 55:16 AMP*

10) He will bring me **safely** back from the battles that **I fight** against so many enemies. — *Psalm 55:18 GNB*

11) **Cast your burden** on the Lord [releasing the weight of it] and **He will sustain you;** He will never allow the [consistently] righteous **to be moved** (made to slip, fall, or fail). — *Psalm 55:22 AMP*

12) but even when I am afraid, **I keep on trusting you.** — *Psalm 56:3 CEV*

13) **I trust in God and am not afraid;** I praise him for what he has promised. What can a mere human being do to me? — *Psalm 56:4 GNB*

14) I am overcome by sorrow; **strengthen me, as you have promised.** — *Psalm 119:28 GNB*

15) Here is a message for all who are weak, trembling, and worried: **"Cheer up! Don't be afraid.** Your God is coming to punish your enemies. **God will take revenge on them and rescue you."** — *Isaiah 35:3-4 CEV*

16) But those who **wait for** the Lord **[who expect, look for, and hope in Him]** shall change and renew their strength and power; they shall lift their wings and mount up [close to God] as eagles [mount up to the sun]; **they shall run and not be weary, they shall walk and not faint** *or* **become tired.** — *Isaiah 40:31 AMP*

17) But no weapon will be able to hurt you; you will have an answer for all who accuse you. I will defend my servants and give them victory." The LORD has spoken. — *Isaiah 54:17 GNB*

18) That's why we boast about you to all of God's churches. We tell them **how patient you are** and **how you keep on having faith,** even though **you are going through a lot of trouble and suffering.** — *2 Thessalonians 1:4 CEV*

19) So whenever we are in need, **we should come bravely before the throne of our merciful God.** There we will be treated with **undeserved kindness, and we will find help.** — *Hebrews 4:16 CEV*

20) Keep your lives free from the love of money, and **be satisfied with what you have.** For God has said, **"I will never leave you; I** will never **abandon you."** — *Hebrews 13:5 GNB*

21) Leave all your worries with him, because he cares for you. — *1 Peter 5:7 GNB*

3d) Faith in God to See You Through
Tough Times

Read On: January 16th | April 2nd | June 18th | September 3rd | November 19th

1) **The LORD is my strong defender; he is the one who has saved me.** He is my God, and I will praise him, my father's God, and I will sing about his greatness. — *Exodus 15:2 GNB*

2) Trust the LORD and his **mighty power. Worship him always.** — *1 Chronicles 16:11 CEV*

3) But you must see that everything is done according to these plans. **Be confident, and never be afraid of anything or get discouraged. The LORD my God will help you do everything needed to finish the temple,** so it can be used for worshiping him. — *1 Chronicles 28:20 CEV*

4) So you must be brave. **Don't give up! God will honour you for obeying him.** — *2 Chronicles 15:7 CEV*

5) But you, O LORD, are **always my shield from danger;** you give me victory and restore my courage. — *Psalm 3:3 GNB*

6) I call to the LORD for help, and from his sacred hill **he answers me.** — *Psalm 3:4 GNB*

7) **I will praise you, LORD, with all my heart;** I will tell of all the wonderful things you have done. — *Psalm 9:1 GNB*

8) The LORD is my **light and my salvation; I will fear no one. The LORD protects me from all danger;** I will never be afraid. — *Psalm 27:1 GNB*

9) Trust the LORD! **Be brave and strong and trust the LORD.** — *Psalm 27:14 CEV*

10) If you obey the LORD, he will watch over you **and answer your prayers.** — *Psalm 34:15 CEV*

11) When his people **pray for help, he listens and rescues them from their troubles.** — *Psalm 34:17 CEV*

12) The LORD's people may suffer a lot, but he will always bring them safely through. — *Psalm 34:19 CEV*

Scripture Therapy Daily Devotional For Men

13) God is our shelter and strength, always ready to help **in times of trouble.** — *Psalm 46:1 GNB*

14) I have **confidence** in your strength; **you are my refuge, O God.** — *Psalm 59:9 GNB*

15) Unto You, O my Strength, I will sing praises; for **God is my Defense, my Fortress,** *and* **High Tower,** the God Who **shows me mercy and steadfast love.** — *Psalm 59:17 AMP*

16) The LORD gives **strength** to those who are weary. — *Isaiah 40:29 CEV*

18) If you are tired from carrying heavy burdens, come to me and I will give you rest. — *Matthew 11:28 CEV*

17) But those who **trust in the LORD** for help **will find their strength renewed.** They will rise on wings like eagles; **they will run and not get weary;** they will walk and not grow weak. — *Isaiah 40:31 GNB*

20) So let us **not become tired** of doing good; **for if we do not give up,** the time will come when **we will reap the harvest.** — *Galatians 6:9 GNB*

19) But his answer was: "My grace is all you need, for my power is greatest when you are weak." I am most happy, then, to be proud of my weaknesses, in order to feel the protection of Christ's power over me. — *2 Corinthians 12:9 GNB*

21) My brothers and sisters, consider yourselves fortunate when all kinds of trials come your way, ³for you know that when your faith succeeds in facing such trials, the result is the ability to endure. — *James 1:2-3 GNB*

22) But you must learn to **endure everything,** so that you will be completely mature and not lacking in anything. — *James 1:4 CEV*

23) God's people must learn to endure. They must also **obey his commands** and **have faith in Jesus.** — *Revelation 14:12 CEV*

51

3e) Conquering Emotional
Stress

Read On: January 17th | April 3rd | June 19th | September 4th | November 20th

1) The LORD said, "I will go with you, and I will give you victory." — *Exodus 33:14 GNB*

2) Be patient and trust the LORD. Don't let it bother you when all goes well for those who do sinful things. — *Psalm 37:7 CEV*

3) Why am I so sad? Why am I so troubled? I will put my hope in God, and once again I will praise him, my saviour and my God. — *Psalm 42:11 GNB*

4) Call to me when trouble comes; I will save you, and you will praise me." — *Psalm 50:15 GNB*

5) Leave your troubles with the LORD, and he will defend you; he never lets honest people be defeated. — *Psalm 55:22 GNB*

6) Without the help of the LORD it is useless to build a home or to guard a city. — *Psalm 127:1 CEV*

7) Lean on, trust in, *and* be confident in the Lord with all your heart *and* mind and do not rely on your own insight or understanding. — *Proverbs 3:5 AMP*

8) Always let him lead you, and he will clear the road for you to follow. — *Proverbs 3:6 CEV*

10) Ask the LORD to bless your plans, and you will be successful in carrying them out. — *Proverbs 16:3 GNB*

9) The LORD will keep you safe. He will not let you fall into a trap. — *Proverbs 3:26 GNB*

11) There is no condemnation now for those who live in union with Christ Jesus. — *Romans 8:1 GNB*

12) We know that God is always at work for the good of everyone who loves him. They are the ones God has chosen for his purpose, — *Romans 8:28 CEV*

Scripture Therapy Daily Devotional For Men

13) In view of all this, what can we say? **If God is for us,** who can be against us — *Romans 8:31 GNB*

14) No, in all these things **we have complete victory through him** who loved us! — *Romans 8:37 GNB*

16) In conclusion, **be strong in the Lord** [be empowered through your union with Him]; **draw your strength from Him** [that strength which His boundless might provides]. — *Ephesians 6:10 AMP*

15) Do not let evil defeat you; instead, conquer evil **with good.** — *Romans 12:21 GNB*

17) God is the one who began this good work in you, and **I am certain that he won't stop before it is complete** on the day that Christ Jesus returns. — *Philippians 1:6 CEV*

18) Consider it wholly joyful, my brethren, whenever you are enveloped in *or* **encounter trials of any sort** *or* **fall into various temptations.** ³Be assured *and* **understand that the trial** *and* **proving of your faith** bring out **endurance** *and* **steadfastness** *and* **patience.** — *James 1:2-3 AMP*

19) So be subject to God. **Resist the devil** [stand firm against him], **and he will flee from you.** — *James 4:7 AMP*

20) And the prayer [that is] of faith will save him who is sick, **and the Lord will restore him;** and if he has committed sins, he will be forgiven. — *James 5:15 AMP*

21) Dear friends, don't be surprised or shocked **that you are going through testing that is like walking through fire.** — *1 Peter 4:12 CEV*

22) If our conscience condemns us, **we know that God is greater than our conscience** and that he knows everything. — *1 John 3:20 GNB*

3f) Encouragement to
Conquer Tough Issues

Read On: January 18th | April 4th | June 20th | September 5th | November 21st

1) We worship you, Lord, and **we should always pray whenever we find out that we have sinned.** Then we won't be swept away by a raging flood. — *Psalm 32:6 CEV*

2) You are my hiding place; **you will save me from trouble.** I sing aloud of your salvation, **because you protect me.** — *Psalm 32:7 GNB*

3) God is our mighty fortress, always ready to help in times of trouble. — *Psalm 46:1 CEV*

4) **God will put his angels in charge** of you **to protect** you wherever you go. — *Psalm 91:11 GNB*

5) He keeps me from the **grave** and blesses me with **love** and **mercy.** — *Psalm 103:4 GNB*

6) You, LORD, will always treat me with kindness. Your love never fails. You have made us what we are. Don't give up on us now! — *Psalm 138:8 CEV*

7) Don't be afraid. I am with you. Don't tremble with fear. I am your God. I will make you strong, as I protect you with my arm and give you victories. — *Isaiah 41:10 CEV*

8) Sing and shout, even though you have never had children! The LORD has promised that you will have more children than someone married for a long time. — *Isaiah 54:1 CEV*

9) But I don't care what happens to me, as long as I finish the work that the Lord Jesus gave me to do. And that work is to tell the good news about God's great kindness. — *Acts 20:24 CEV*

10) There is no condemnation now for those who live in union with Christ Jesus. — *Romans 8:1 GNB*

Scripture Therapy Daily Devotional For Men

11) You were saved **by faith in God,** who treats us **much better than we deserve.** This is **God's gift to you,** and not anything **you have done on your own.** ⁹It isn't something you have earned, so there is nothing you can boast about. — *Ephesians 2:8-9 CEV*

12) God planned for us to do **good things** and to live **as he has always wanted us to live.** That's why **he sent Christ to make us what we are.** — *Ephesians 2:10 CEV*

13) Whatever happens, keep thanking God because of Jesus Christ. This is what God **wants you to do.** — *1 Thessalonians 5:18 CEV*

14) For the Spirit that God has given us **does not make us timid;** instead, his **Spirit fills us with power, love, and self-control.** — *2 Timothy 1:7 GNB*

15) As for you, my son, **be strong through the grace** that is ours **in union with Christ Jesus.** — *2 Timothy 2:1 GNB*

16) Let us then **fearlessly** and **confidently** and **boldly** draw near to the throne of grace **(the throne of God's unmerited favor to us sinners),** that we may receive **mercy [for our failures]** and find **grace to help** in good time **for every need** [appropriate help and well-timed help, **coming just when we need it].** — *Hebrews 4:16 AMP*

17) So get rid of every **filthy habit** and all **wicked conduct.** Submit to God and **accept the word** that he plants **in your hearts,** which is **able to save you.** — *James 1:21 GNB*

18) Therefore **humble** yourselves **[demote, lower yourselves in your own estimation]** under the mighty hand of God, that in due time He may exalt you. — *1 Peter 5:6 AMP*

19) I pray that God will be kind to you and will let you live in perfect peace! May you keep learning more and more about **God and our Lord Jesus.** — *2 Peter 1:2 CEV*

20) Let the **wonderful kindness** and the **understanding** that come from **our Lord and Savior Jesus Christ** help **you to keep on growing.** Praise Jesus now and forever! Amen. — *2 Peter 3:18 CEV*

CHAPTER 4

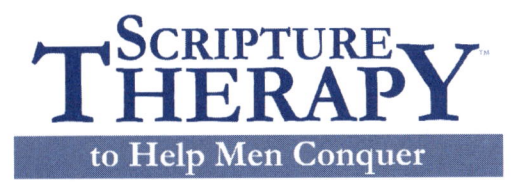

Scripture Therapy™ to Help Men Conquer
Addiction Issues

TOPICS

4a) Conquering The Urge to Give in to Temptation
Read On: January 19th | April 5th | June 21st | September 6th | November 22nd

4b) Conquering Addictions and Bad Habits
Read On: January 20th | April 6th | June 22nd | September 7th | November 23rd

4c) The Lord's Help Conquering Addictions
Read On: January 21st | April 7th | June 23rd | September 8th | November 24th

4d) Conquering Addiction to Pornography
Read On: January 22nd | April 8th | June 24th | September 9th | November 25th

4e) Conquering Addiction to Masturbation
Read On: January 23rd | April 9th | June 25th | September 10th | November 26th

4f) Conquering Sexual Unfaithfulness
Read On: January 24th | April 10th | June 26th | September 11th | November 27th

4g) Conquering Lust and Harmful Sexual Addictions
Read On: January 25th | April 11th | June 27th | September 12th | November 28th

4h) Conquering Addiction to Alcohol or Drugs
Read On: January 26th | April 12th | June 28th | September 13th | November 29th

57

4a) Conquering The Urge To Give In To
Temptation

Read On: January 19th | April 5th | June 21st | September 6th | November 22nd

1) But I trust the LORD God to save me, and I will wait for him to answer my prayer. — *Micah 7:7 CEV*

2) God blesses those people who refuse evil advice and won't follow sinners or join in sneering at God. — *Psalm 1:1 CEV*

3) Hear me, LORD, when I call to you! Be merciful and answer me! — *Psalm 27:7 GNB*

4) Teach me, LORD, what you want me to do, and I will obey you faithfully; teach me to serve you with complete devotion. *-Psalm 86:11 GNB*

5) I look to the mountains; where will my help come from? ²My help will come from the LORD, who made heaven and earth. — *Psalm 121:1-2 GNB*

6) When sinners tempt you, my son, don't give in. — *Proverbs 1:10 GNB*

7) Stay awake and pray that you won't be tested. You want to do what is right, but you are weak." — *Matthew 26:41 CEV*

8) In certain ways we are weak, but the Spirit is here to help us. For example, when we don't know what to pray for, the Spirit prays for us in ways that cannot be put into words. — *Romans 8:26 CEV*

9) And God, who sees into our hearts, knows what the thought of the Spirit is; because the Spirit pleads with God on behalf of his people *and* in accordance with his will. — *Romans 8:27 GNB*

10) Do not be conformed to this world (this age), [fashioned after and adapted to its external, superficial customs], but be transformed (changed) by the [entire] renewal of your mind [by its new ideals and its new attitude], so that you may prove [for yourselves] what is the good and acceptable and perfect will of God, *even the thing which is good and acceptable and* perfect [in His sight for you]. — *Romans 12:2 AMP*

Scripture Therapy Daily Devotional For Men

11) **Don't you know that your body is the temple of the Holy Spirit,** who lives in you and who was given to you by God? **You do not belong to yourselves but to God;** — *1 Corinthians 6:19 GNB*

12) Even if you think **you can stand up to temptation, be careful not to fall.** — *1 Corinthians 10:12 CEV*

13) **You are tempted in the same way that everyone else is tempted.** But God can be trusted not to let you be tempted too much, and **he will show you how to escape from your temptations.** — *1 Corinthians 10:13 CEV*

14) In conclusion, my brothers and sisters, **fill your minds with those things that are good** and that deserve praise: **things that are true, noble, right, pure, lovely, and honourable.** — *Philippians 4:8 GNB*

15) **I have the strength to face all conditions** by the power that Christ gives me. — *Philippians 4:13 GNB*

16) **The love of money causes all kinds of trouble.** Some people **want money so much** that they have given up their faith and caused themselves **a lot of pain.** — *1 Timothy 6:10 CEV*

17) My brothers and sisters, consider yourselves fortunate when all kinds of trials come your way, ³for you know **that when your faith succeeds in facing such trials,** the result is **the ability to endure.** — *James 1:2-3 GNB*

18) **If people are tempted by such trials,** they must not say, "This temptation comes from God." **For God cannot be tempted by evil, and he himself tempts no one.** — *James 1:13 GNB*

19) **We are tempted by our own desires** that drag us off and **trap us.** — *James 1:14 CEV*

20) **Our desires make us sin,** and when sin is finished with us, it leaves us dead. ¹⁶**Don't be fooled, my dear friends.** — *James 1:15-16 CEV*

21) **Surrender to God! Resist the** devil, and he will run from you. — *James 4:7 CEV*

22) **Be alert and think straight.** Put all your hope **in how kind God will be to you** when Jesus Christ appears. — *1 Peter 1:13 CEV*

23) My dear friends, **do not be surprised at the painful test you are suffering,** as though something unusual were happening to you. — *1 Peter 4:12 GNB*

4b) Conquering
Addictions and Bad Habits

Read On: January 20th | April 6th | June 22nd | September 7th | November 23rd

1) I treasure your word above all else; it keeps me from sinning against you. —*Psalm 119:11 CEV*

2) But seek (aim at and strive after) first of all His kingdom and His righteousness (His way of doing and being right), and then all these things taken together will be given you besides. —*Matthew 6:33 AMP*

3) What should we say? Should we keep on sinning, so that God's wonderful kindness will show up even better? —*Romans 6:1 CEV*

4) I appeal to you therefore, brethren, *and* beg of you in view of [all] the mercies of God, to make a decisive dedication of your bodies [presenting all your members and faculties] as a living sacrifice, holy (devoted, consecrated) *and* well pleasing to God, which is your reasonable (rational, intelligent) service *and* spiritual worship. —*Romans 12:1 AMP*

5) Don't be like the people of this world, but let God change the way you think. Then you will know how to do everything that is good and pleasing to him. —*Romans 12:2 CEV*

6) Let the Lord Jesus Christ be as near to you as the clothes you wear. Then you won't try to satisfy your selfish desires. —*Romans 13:14 CEV*

7) Some of you say, "We can do anything we want to." But I tell you that not everything is good for us. So I refuse to let anything have power over me. —*1 Corinthians 6:12 CEV*

8) Don't be immoral in matters of sex. That is a sin against your own body in a way that no other sin is. —*1 Corinthians 6:18 CEV*

9) Actually all of us were like them and lived according to our natural desires, doing whatever suited the wishes of our own bodies and minds. In our natural condition we, like everyone else, were destined to suffer God's anger. —*Ephesians 2:3 GNB*

Scripture Therapy Daily Devotional For Men

10) You were told that your foolish desires will destroy you and that you must give up your old way of life with all its bad habits. —*Ephesians 4:22 CEV*

11) Since you are God's dear children, you must try to be like him. —*Ephesians 5:1 GNB*

12) So put on God's armour now! Then when the evil day comes, you will be able to resist the enemy's attacks; and after fighting to the end, you will still hold your ground. —*Ephesians 6:13 GNB*

14) So get rid of every filthy habit and all wicked conduct. Submit to God and accept the word that he plants in your hearts, which is able to save you. —*James 1:21 GNB*

13) Such a large crowd of witnesses is all around us! So we must get rid of everything that slows us down, especially the sin that just won't let go. And we must be determined to run the race that is ahead of us. —*Hebrews 12:1 CEV*

16) Rid yourselves, then, of all evil; no more lying or hypocrisy or jealousy or insulting language. —*1 Peter 2:1 GNB*

15) Behave like obedient children. Don't let your lives be controlled by your desires, as they used to be. —*1 Peter 1:14 CEV*

17) Be on your guard and stay awake. Your enemy, the devil, is like a roaring lion, prowling around to find someone to attack. ⁹But you must resist the devil and stay strong in your faith. You know that all over the world the Lord's followers are suffering just as you are. —*1 Peter 5:8-9 CEV*

18) If we [freely] admit that we have sinned and confess our sins, He is faithful and just (true to His own nature and promises) and will forgive our sins [dismiss our lawlessness] and [continuously] cleanse us from all unrighteousness [everything not in conformity to His will in purpose, thought, and action]. —*1 John 1:9 AMP*

19) I am writing to you, my children, because you know the Father. I am writing to you, fathers, because you know him who has existed from the beginning. I am writing to you, young people, because you are strong; the word of God lives in you, and you have defeated the Evil One. —*1 John 2:14 GNB*

4c) The Lord's Help
Conquering Addictions

Read On: January 21ˢᵗ | April 7ᵗʰ | June 23ʳᵈ | September 8ᵗʰ | November 24ᵗʰ

1) You will not have to fight this battle. **Just take up your positions and wait; you will see the LORD give you victory.** People of Judah and Jerusalem, do not **hesitate** or be **afraid.** Go out to battle, and the LORD will be with you!" — *2 Chronicles 20:17 GNB*

2) **With wisdom you will learn what is right** and honest and fair. — *Proverbs 2:9 CEV*

3) Don't ever think that you are wise enough, **but respect the LORD and stay away from evil.** — *Proverbs 3:7 CEV*

4) If you don't confess your sins, you will be a failure. **But God will be merciful if you confess your sins and give them up.** — *Proverbs 28:13 CEV*

5) **Do not be afraid — I am with you!** I am your God — let nothing terrify you! **I will make you strong and help you; I will protect you and save you.** — *Isaiah 41:10 GNB*

6) **If you are tired** from carrying **heavy burdens,** come to me and **I will give you rest.** — *Matthew 11:28 CEV*

7) Behold! **I have given you authority and power** to trample upon serpents and scorpions, and [physical and mental strength and ability] over all the power that the enemy [possesses]; and nothing shall in any way harm you. — *Luke 10:19 AMP*

8) Jesus told his disciples a story about **how they should keep on praying and never give up.** — *Luke 18:1 CEV*

9) **Stay joined to me, and I will stay joined to you.** Just as a branch cannot produce fruit unless it stays joined to the vine, **you cannot produce fruit unless you stay joined to me.** — *John 15:4 CEV*

10) I am the vine, and you are the branches. **If you stay joined to me,** and **I stay joined to you,** then you will produce lots of fruit. But you cannot do anything without me. — *John 15:5 CEV*

Scripture Therapy Daily Devotional For Men

11) Therefore, [there is] now no condemnation (no adjudging guilty of wrong) for those who are in Christ Jesus, who live [and] walk not after the dictates of the flesh, but after the dictates of the Spirit. — *Romans 8:1 AMP*

12) We know that **God is always at work for the good of everyone who loves him.** They are the ones God has chosen for his purpose. — *Romans 8:28 CEV*

13) We often suffer, but we are never crushed. Even when we don't know what to do, we never give up. — *2 Corinthians 4:8 CEV*

14) Now to Him Who, by (in consequence of) the [action of His] power that **is at work within us, is able to [carry out His purpose and] do superabundantly, far over** *and* **above all that we [dare] ask or think** [infinitely beyond our highest prayers, desires, thoughts, hopes, or dreams] — *Ephesians 3:20 AMP*

15) Let your faith be like a shield, **and you will be able to stop all the flaming arrows** of the evil one. — *Ephesians 6:16 CEV*

16) God is the one who began this good work in you, **and I am certain that he won't stop before it is complete** on the day that Christ Jesus returns. — *Philippians 1:6 CEV*

17) Don't worry about anything, **but pray about everything. With thankful hearts offer up your prayers** and requests **to God.** — *Philippians 4:6 CEV*

18) God rescued us from the dark power of Satan and brought us **into the kingdom** of his dear Son. — *Colossians 1:13 CEV*

19) So if you don't obey these rules, you are not really disobeying us. **You are disobeying God,** who gives you his Holy Spirit. — *1 Thessalonians 4:8 CEV*

20) Let us then **fearlessly** *and* **confidently** *and* **boldly** draw near to the throne of grace **(the throne of God's unmerited favor to us sinners),** that we may **receive mercy** [for our failures] and find **grace to help in good time for every need** [appropriate help and well-timed help, **coming just when we need it].** — *Hebrews 4:16 AMP*

21) Jesus understands every weakness of ours, because he was tempted in every way that we are. **But he did not sin!** — *Hebrews 4:15 CEV*

22) If our conscience condemns us, we know that **God is greater than our conscience** and that he knows everything. — *1 John 3:20 GNB*

63

4d) Conquering Addiction to
Pornography

Read On: January 22nd | April 8th | June 24th | September 9th | November 25th

1) I have made a solemn promise **never to look with lust at a woman.** — *Job 31:1 GNB*

2) **Don't let me do wrong on purpose, Lord, or let sin have control over my life.** Then I will be innocent, and not guilty of some terrible fault. — *Psalm 19:13 CEV*

4) How can young people keep their lives **pure? By obeying your commands.** — *Psalm 119:9 GNB*

3) **I will set no base or wicked thing before my eyes.** I hate the work of them who turn aside [from the right path]; **it shall not grasp hold of me.** — *Psalm 101:3 AMP*

5) Avoid it, do not go on it; turn from it and pass on. — *Proverbs 4:15 AMP*

6) Why should you, my son, **be infatuated with a loose woman,** embrace the bosom of an outsider, and go astray? — *Proverbs 5:20 AMP*

7) They will no longer worship idols **and do things that make them unacceptable to me.** I will wash away their sin and **make them clean,** and I will **protect them from everything that makes them unclean.** They will be my people, and I will be their God. — *Ezekiel 37:23 CEV*

8) "The priests are to **teach my people the difference** between **what is holy** and **what is not,** and between what is **ritually clean** and what is not. — *Ezekiel 44:23 GNB*

9) But I tell you that if you **look at another woman and want her,** you are already **unfaithful** in your **thoughts.** — *Matthew 5:28 CEV*

10) Do not conform yourselves to the **standards** of this world, but let God **transform** you inwardly by a **complete change** of your mind. Then you will be able to know the **will of God** — what is **good** and is **pleasing to him** and is perfect. — *Romans 12:2 GNB*

11) Even if you think you can stand up to temptation, **be careful not to fall.** — *1 Corinthians 10:12 CEV*

64

Scripture Therapy Daily Devotional For Men

12) You are tempted in the same way that **everyone else is tempted.** But God can be trusted **not to let you be tempted too much,** and he will show you how to escape from your temptations. — *1 Corinthians 10:13 CEV*

13) And so the Lord says, "You must **leave them and separate yourselves** from them. **Have nothing to do with what is unclean,** and I will **accept** you. — *2 Corinthians 6:17 GNB*

14) And **do not make God's Holy Spirit sad;** for the Spirit is God's mark of ownership on you, a guarantee that the Day will come when God will set you free. — *Ephesians 4:30 GNB*

15) You are God's people, so don't let it be said that any of you are **immoral** or **indecent** or **greedy.** — *Ephesians 5:3 CEV*

16) Finally, my friends, **keep your minds on whatever is true, pure, right, holy, friendly,** and **proper.** Don't ever stop thinking about what is truly **worthwhile** and **worthy of praise.** — *Philippians 4:8 CEV*

17) God wants you to be holy, **so don't be immoral in matters of sex.** — *1 Thessalonians 4:3 CEV*

18) Abstain from evil [shrink from it and keep aloof from it] in **whatever form** *or* **whatever kind it may be.** — *1 Thessalonians 5:22 AMP*

19) Avoid the passions of youth, and **strive for righteousness, faith, love,** *and* peace, together with those who with a **pure heart call out to the Lord for help.** — *2 Timothy 2:22 GNB*

20) Instead, in order that **none of you be deceived by sin** and become stubborn, **you must help one another every day,** as long as the word "Today" in the scripture applies to us. — *Hebrews 3:13 GNB*

21) God will bless you, **if you don't give up when your faith is being tested.** He will reward you with a **glorious life,** just as **he rewards everyone who loves him.** — *James 1:12 CEV*

22) [Live] as children of obedience [to God]; do not conform yourselves to the evil desires [that governed you] in your former ignorance [when you did not know the requirements of the Gospel]. — *1 Peter 1:14 AMP*

23) But if we **claim** to know him **and don't obey him,** we are **lying** and the truth isn't in our hearts. — *1 John 2:4 CEV*

4e) Conquering Addiction to
Masturbation

Read On: January 23rd | April 9th | June 25th | September 10th | November 26th

1) "Tell me," Samuel said. "Does the LORD really want sacrifices and offerings? **No! He doesn't want your sacrifices. He wants you to obey him.** — *1 Samuel 15:22 CEV*

2) And you shall be holy to Me; for I the Lord am holy, and have **separated you from the peoples,** that you should be **Mine.** — *Leviticus 20:26 AMP*

3) I treasure your word above all else; **it keeps me from sinning against you.** — *Psalm 119:11 CEV*

4) You are all I want, O LORD; I promise to obey your laws. 58**I ask you with all my heart to have mercy on me, as you have promised!** 59**I have considered my conduct, and I promise to follow your instructions.** — *Psalm 119:57-59 GNB*

5) The LORD sees everything you do. Wherever you go, **he is watching.** — *Proverbs 5:21 GNB*

6) Keep watch and pray that you will not fall into temptation. The spirit is willing, but the flesh is weak." — *Matthew 26:41 GNB*

7) Sin must no longer rule in your mortal bodies, **so that you obey the desires of your natural self.** — *Romans 6:12 GNB*

8) Nor must you surrender any part of yourselves to sin to be used for wicked purposes. Instead, give yourselves to God, as those who have been brought from death to life, and **surrender your whole being to him to be used for righteous purposes.** — *Romans 6:13 GNB*

9) In fact, I don't understand why I act the way I do. I don't do what I know is **right.** I do the things **I hate.** — *Romans 7:15 CEV*

10) He will also keep you firm to the end, so that you will be **faultless** on the Day of our Lord Jesus Christ. — *1 Corinthians 1:8 GNB*

11) Don't be immoral in matters of sex. That is a sin **against your own body** in a way that no other sin is. — *1 Corinthians 6:18 CEV*

Scripture Therapy Daily Devotional For Men

12) But if you don't have enough self-control, **then go ahead and get married.** After all, **it is better to marry than to burn with desire.** — *1 Corinthians 7:9 CEV*

13) My friends, God has made us these promises. **So we should stay away from everything that keeps our bodies and spirits from being clean.** We should honour God and try to be completely **like him.** — *2 Corinthians 7:1 CEV*

14) God is working in you to make you **willing** and **able** to **obey** him. — *Philippians 2:13 CEV*

15) That **each one of you** should know how to possess (control, manage) **his own body** in consecration (purity, separated from things profane) and honor, — *1 Thessalonians 4:4 AMP*

16) That's also how it is with people. **The ones who stop doing evil and make themselves pure will become special.** Their lives will be holy and **pleasing to their Master,** and they will be **able to do** all kinds of **good deeds.** — *2 Timothy 2:21 CEV*

17) Learn to be patient, so that you will **please God** and be given **what he has promised.** — *Hebrews 10:36 CEV*

18) Such a large crowd of witnesses is all around us! **So we must get rid of everything that slows us down, especially the sin that just won't let go.** And we must be determined to run the race that is ahead of us. — *Hebrews 12:1 CEV*

19) I appeal to you, my friends, as strangers and refugees in this world! **Do not give in to bodily passions,** which are **always at war against the soul.** — *1 Peter 2:11 GNB*

20) But if we **confess our sins to God,** he can **always be trusted to forgive us** and **take our sins away.** — *1 John 1:9 CEV*

21) Everyone who has this hope in Christ **keeps himself pure,** just as **Christ is pure.** — *1 John 3:3 GNB*

67

4f) Conquering Sexual Unfaithfulness

Read On: January 24th | April 10th | June 26th | September 11th | November 27th

1) Never let yourself **think that you are wiser** than you are; **simply obey the Lord** and **refuse to do wrong.** — *Proverbs 3:7 GNB*

2) Don't go mad **over a woman who is unfaithful** to her own husband! — *Proverbs 5:20 CEV*

3) **Don't let yourself be attracted** by the charm and lovely eyes **of someone like that.** — *Proverbs 6:25 CEV*

4) A woman who **sells her love** can be bought for as little as the price of a meal. **But making love to another man's wife will cost you everything.** — *Proverbs 6:26 CEV*

5) But if you go to bed with another man's wife, **you will destroy yourself by your own stupidity.** [33]**You will be beaten and for ever disgraced.** — *Proverbs 6:32-33 CEV*

6) **Remember what I say, my son,** and **never forget what I tell you to do.** — *Proverbs 7:1 GNB*

7) **Do what I say,** and you will live. **Be as careful to follow my teaching** as you are to protect your eyes. — *Proverbs 7:2 GNB*

8) They will **keep you away** from other men's wives, **from women with seductive words.** — *Proverbs 7:5 GNB*

9) **Don't even think about that kind of woman** or let yourself be misled by someone like her. — *Proverbs 7:25 CEV*

10) **If you go to her house,** you are on the way to the world of the dead. **It is a short cut to death.** — *Proverbs 7:27 GNB*

11) **If you respect the Lord,** you will live longer; **if you keep doing wrong,** your life will be cut short. — *Proverbs 10:27 CEV*

12) **If you reject God's teaching,** you will pay the price; **if you obey his commands,** you will be **rewarded.** — *Proverbs 13:13 CEV*

Scripture Therapy Daily Devotional For Men

13) Someone who will **not learn** will be poor and disgraced. **Anyone who listens to correction** is respected. — *Proverbs 13:18 GNB*

14) Obey the LORD and **you will live a long life,** content and safe from harm. — *Proverbs 19:23 GNB*

15) If you love your life, **stay away from the traps that catch the wicked** along the way. — *Proverbs 22:5 GNB*

16) Prostitutes and **immoral women** are a deadly **trap.** — *Proverbs 23:27 GNB*

17) They wait for you like robbers and **cause many men to be unfaithful.** — *Proverbs 23:28 GNB*

18) Enjoy life with the **woman you love,** as long as you live the useless life that God has given you in this world. **Enjoy every useless day of it,** because that is **all you will get** for all your trouble. — *Ecclesiastes 9:9 GNB*

19) Avoid Immorality. Any other sin a man commits does not affect his body; **but the man who is guilty of sexual immorality sins against his own body.** — *1 Corinthians 6:18 GNB*

20) But because of the **temptation to impurity** *and* to avoid immorality, let each [man] **have his own wife** and let each [woman] **have her own husband.** — *1 Corinthians 7:2 AMP*

21) A man should **fulfil his duty as a husband,** and a woman should **fulfil her duty as a wife,** and **each should satisfy the other's needs.** — *1 Corinthians 7:3 GNB*

22) So don't refuse sex to each other, unless you agree not to have sex for a little while, in order to spend time in prayer. Then Satan **won't be able to tempt you because of your lack of self-control.** — *1 Corinthians 7:5 CEV*

23) Have **respect for marriage. Always be faithful to your partner,** because God will punish anyone who is **immoral or unfaithful in marriage.** — *Hebrews 13:4 CEV*

24) So any person **who knows** what is **right** to do but **does not do it,** to him it is sin. — *James 4:17 AMP*

4g) Conquering Lust and Harmful
Sexual Addictions

Read On: January 25th | April 11th | June 27th | September 12th | November 28th

1) **The words of an immoral woman** may be as sweet as honey and as smooth as olive oil. — *Proverbs 5:3 CEV*

2) but when it is all over, **she leaves you nothing but bitterness and pain.** — *Proverbs 5:4 GNB*

3) **Keep away from such a woman! Don't even go near her door!** — *Proverbs 5:8 GNB*

4) **If you do, others will gain the respect that you once had,** and you will die young at the hands of merciless people. — *Proverbs 5:9 GNB*

5) **Yes, strangers will take all your wealth,** and what you have worked for will belong to someone else. — *Proverbs 5:10 GNB*

6) and you will say, **"Why would I never learn? Why would I never let anyone correct me?"** — *Proverbs 5:12 GNB*

7) **I wouldn't listen** to my teachers. **I paid no attention** to them. ¹⁴And suddenly I found **myself publicly disgraced.** — *Proverbs 5:13-14 GNB*

8) **Be faithful to your own wife** and give your love to her alone. — *Proverbs 5:15 GNB*

9) And don't be like a stream from which **just any woman may take a drink.** — *Proverbs 5:16 CEV*

10) **So be happy with your wife** and find your joy **with the woman you married.** — *Proverbs 5:18 GNB*

11) **Don't spend all your energy on sex** and all your money **on women;** they have **destroyed kings.** — *Proverbs 31:3 GNB*

12) But clothe yourself with the Lord Jesus Christ (the Messiah), **and make no provision for [indulging] the flesh [put a stop to thinking about the evil cravings of your physical nature]** to [gratify its] desires **(lusts).** — *Romans 13:14 AMP*

70

13) Some of you say, "We can do anything we want to." But I tell you that **not everything is good for us.** So **I refuse to let anything have power over me.** — *1 Corinthians 6:12 CEV*

14) I harden my body with blows **and bring it under complete control, to keep myself from being disqualified** after having called **others** to the contest. — *1 Corinthians 9:27 GNB*

15) As a follower of the Lord, I order you to stop living like stupid, godless people. ¹⁸Their minds are in the dark, and they are **stubborn** and ignorant and have missed out on the life that **comes from God. They no longer have any feelings about what is right.** — *Ephesians 4:17-18 CEV*

16) They have lost all feeling of shame; they give themselves over to vice and do all sorts of **indecent things without restraint.** — *Ephesians 4:19 GNB*

17) You were told that your foolish desires will destroy you and that **you must give up your old way of life with all its bad habits.** — *Ephesians 4:22 CEV*

18) Your **hearts** and **minds** must be made **completely new.** — *Ephesians 4:23 GNB*

19) Don't give the Devil a chance. — *Ephesians 4:27 GNB*

20) He taught us to give up our wicked ways and our worldly desires and to live **decent and honest** lives in this world. — *Titus 2:12 CEV*

21) I appeal to you, my friends, as strangers and refugees in this world! **Do not give in to bodily passions, which are always at war against the soul.** — *1 Peter 2:11 GNB*

22) Be alert, be on the watch! Your enemy, the Devil, roams round like a roaring lion, **looking for someone to devour.** ⁹**Be firm in your faith and resist him,** because you know that **your fellow-believers in all the world are going through the same kind of sufferings.** — *1 Peter 5:8-9 GNB*

4h) Conquering Addiction to
Alcohol or Drugs

Read On: January 26th | April 12th | June 28th | September 13th | November 29th

1) **Drinking too much** makes you **loud** and **foolish. It's stupid to get drunk.** *—Proverbs 20:1 GNB*

2) **Heavy drinkers** and others who live only for pleasure **will lose all they have.** *— Proverbs 21:17 CEV*

3) Listen to me, my children! **Be wise** and **have enough sense to follow the right path.** *— Proverbs 23:19 CEV*

4) **Don't be a heavy drinker** or **stuff yourself with food.** 21It will make you feel drowsy, **and you will end up poor** with only rags to wear. *— Proverbs 23:20-21 CEV*

5) Show me someone who **drinks too much, who has to try out some new drink,** and I will show you someone miserable and sorry for himself, **always causing trouble** and always complaining. His eyes are bloodshot, **and he has bruises that could have been avoided.** *—Proverbs 23:29-30 GNB*

6) **Don't let wine tempt you,** even though it is rich red, though it sparkles in the cup, **and it goes down smoothly.** *— Proverbs 23:31 GNB*

7) The next morning you will feel as if you had been bitten by a poisonous snake. 33Weird sights will appear before your eyes, and you will not be able to think or speak clearly. 34You will feel as if you were out on the ocean, sea-sick, swinging high up in the rigging of a tossing ship. 35"I must have been hit," you will say; "I must have been beaten up, but I don't remember it. Why can't I wake up? I need another drink." *— Proverbs 23:32-35 GNB*

8) A fool quoting a wise saying reminds you of **a drunk trying to pick a thorn out of his hand.** *— Proverbs 26:9 GNB*

9) An employer who hires **any fool that comes along** is only **hurting everybody concerned.** *— Proverbs 26:10 GNB*

10) Listen, Lemuel. **Kings should not drink wine or have a craving for alcohol.** *— Proverbs 31:4 GNB*

11) When they drink, they forget the laws and ignore the rights of people in need. — *Proverbs 31:5 GNB*

12) But a nation will prosper when its ruler is mature, and its leaders don't feast too much. — *Ecclesiastes 10:17 CEV*

13) So behave properly, as people do in the day. Don't go to wild parties or get drunk or be vulgar or indecent. Don't quarrel or be jealous. — *Romans 13:13 CEV*

14) What I meant was that you should not associate with a person who calls himself a believer but is immoral or greedy or worships idols or is a slanderer or a drunkard or a thief. Don't even sit down to eat with such a person. — *1 Corinthians 5:11 GNB*

15) If you are guided by the Spirit, you won't obey your selfish desires. — *Galatians 5:16 CEV*

16) People's desires make them give in to immoral ways, filthy thoughts, and shameful deeds. — *Galatians 5:19 CEV*

17) They get drunk, carry on at wild parties, and do other evil things as well. I told you before, and I am telling you again: no one who does these things will share in the blessings of God's kingdom. — *Galatians 5:21 CEV*

18) My friends, you are spiritual. So if someone is trapped in sin, you should gently lead that person back to the right path. But watch out, and don't be tempted yourself. — *Galatians 6:1 CEV*

19) Once we were also ruled by the selfish desires of our bodies and minds. We had made God angry, and we were going to be punished like everyone else. — *Ephesians 2:3 CEV*

20) Don't destroy yourself by getting drunk, but let the Spirit fill your life. — *Ephesians 5:18 CEV*

21) Women must also be serious. **They must not gossip or be heavy drinkers,** and they must be faithful in everything they do.
— *1 Timothy 3:11 CEV*

22) But if we claim to know him and don't obey him, **we are lying** and the truth isn't **in our hearts.**
—*1 John 2:4 CEV*

23) **We truly love God only when we obey him as we should,** and then we know that we belong to him.
— *1 John 2:5 CEV*

24) This hope makes us keep ourselves holy, **just as Christ is holy.**
— *1 John 3:3 CEV*

CHAPTER 5

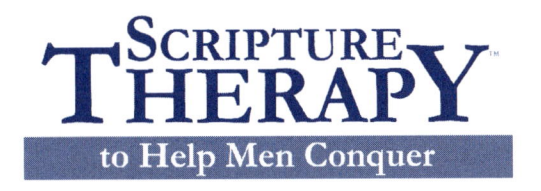

Scripture Therapy
to Help Men Conquer
Financial Issues

TOPICS

5a) Being Faithful to The Lord With Your Finances
Read On: January 27th | April 13th | June 29th | September 14th | November 30th

5b) Conquering Selfishness by Being Generous
Read On: January 28th | April 14th | June 30th | September 15th | December 1st

5c) Conquering Your Financial Struggles
Read On: January 29th | April 15th | July 1st | September 16th | December 2nd

5d) Having Enough Money to Meet Your Needs
Read On: January 30th | April 16th | July 2nd | September 17th | December 3rd

5e) Conquering Poverty and Lack
Read On: January 31st | April 17th | July 3rd | September 18th | December 4th

5a) Being Faithful to The Lord With
Your Finances

Read On: January 27th | April 13th | June 29th | September 14th | November 30th

1) You shall surely tithe all the yield of your seed produced by your field each year. — *Deuteronomy 14:22 AMP*

3) Honour the Lord by giving him your money and the first part of all your crops. — *Proverbs 3:9 CEV*

4) Then you will have more grain and grapes than you will ever need. — *Proverbs 3:10 CEV*

5) Respect and serve the Lord! Your reward will be wealth, a long life, and honour. — *Proverbs 22:4 CEV*

6) Selfish people cause trouble, but you will live a full life if you trust the Lord. — *Proverbs 28:25 CEV*

7) Descendants of Jacob, I am the Lord All-Powerful, and I never change. That's why you haven't been wiped out, [7]even though you have ignored and disobeyed my laws ever since the time of your ancestors. But if you return to me, I will return to you. And yet you ask, "How can we return?" — *Malachi 3:6-7 CEV*

2) say to the LORD, 'None of the sacred tithe is left in my house; I have given it to the Levites, the foreigners, the orphans, and the widows, as you commanded me to do. I have not disobeyed or forgotten any of your commands concerning the tithe. [14]I have not eaten any of it when I was mourning; I have not taken any of it out of my house when I was ritually unclean; and I have not given any of it as an offering for the dead. I have obeyed you, O LORD; I have done everything you commanded concerning the tithe. — *Deuteronomy 26:13-14 GNB*

8) You people are robbing me, your God. And, here you are, asking, "How are we robbing you?" You are robbing me of the offerings and of the ten percent that belongs to me. — *Malachi 3:8 CEV*

9) I am the LORD All-Powerful, and I challenge you to put me to the test. Bring the **entire ten per cent into the storehouse,** so there will be food in my house. **Then I will open the windows of heaven and flood you with blessing after blessing.** — *Malachi 3:10 CEV*

10) I will also stop locusts from destroying your crops and keeping your vineyards from producing. ¹²Everyone of every nation will talk about how I have blessed you and about your wonderful land. I, the LORD All-Powerful, have spoken! — *Malachi 3:11-12 CEV*

11) But more than anything else, **put God's work first and do what he wants.** Then the other things will **be yours as well.** — *Matthew 6:33 CEV*

12) Anyone who can be trusted in little matters can also be trusted in important matters. But anyone who is **dishonest** in little matters will be dishonest in **important** matters. — *Luke 16:10 CEV*

13) We have sown spiritual seed among you. **Is it too much if we reap material benefits from you?** — *1 Corinthians 9:11 GNB*

14) Do you not know that **those men who are employed in the services of the temple get their food from the temple?** And that those who tend the altar **share with the altar** [in the offerings brought]? — *1 Corinthians 9:13 AMP*

15) In the same way, **the Lord has ordered** that **those who preach the gospel** should get their **living from it.** — *1 Corinthians 9:14 GNB*

16) For, as the scripture says, **"The earth and everything in it belong to the Lord."** — *1 Corinthians 10:26 GNB*

17) So I thought it was necessary to urge these brothers and sisters to go to you ahead of me and **get ready in advance the gift you promised to make.** Then it will be ready when I arrive, **and it will show that you give because you want to, not because you have to.** — *2 Corinthians 9:5 GNB*

18) [Remember] this: he who sows **sparingly** and **grudgingly will also reap sparingly** and **grudgingly,** and he who sows **generously** [that blessings may come to someone] **will also reap generously** and with blessings. — *2 Corinthians 9:6 AMP*

19) Each of you must make up your own mind about **how much to give.** But don't feel sorry that you must give and **don't feel that you are forced to give. God loves people who love to give.** — *2 Corinthians 9:7 CEV*

20) And God is able to give you **more than you need,** so that **you will always have all you need for yourselves** and more than enough **for every good cause.** — *2 Corinthians 9:8 GNB*

21) As the scripture says: "**He gives generously to the needy;** his kindness lasts forever." — *2 Corinthians 9:9 GNB*

22) God gives seed to farmers and provides everyone with food. **He will increase what you have, so that you can give even more to those in need.** — *2 Corinthians 9:10 CEV*

23) He will always **make you rich enough to be generous at all times,** so that many will thank God for your gifts which they receive from us. — *2 Corinthians 9:11 GNB*

24) Those who are being **taught** the Christian message **should share all the good things they have with their teachers.** — *Galatians 6:6 GNB*

5b) Conquering Selfishness by Being Generous

Read On: January 28th | April 14th | June 30th | September 15th | December 1st

1) Isaac planted grain **and had a good harvest that same year. The Lord blessed him.** — *Genesis 26:12 CEV*

2) I am old now; I have lived a long time, **but I have never seen good people abandoned by the LORD or their children begging for food.** — *Psalm 37:25 GNB*

3) At all times **they give freely and lend to others,** and their children are a blessing. — *Psalm 37:26 GNB*

4) Life will go well for those **who freely lend and are honest in business.** — *Psalm 112:5 CEV*

5) A good person will never fail; he will always be **remembered.** — *Psalm 112:6 GNB*

6) He gives generously to the needy, and his kindness never fails; **he will be powerful and respected.** — *Psalm 112:9 GNB*

7) **Sometimes you can become rich by being generous** or poor by being greedy. — *Proverbs 11:24 CEV*

8) **Generosity will be rewarded:** Give a cup of water, **and you will receive** a cup of water in return. — *Proverbs 11:25 CEV*

9) If you know what you're doing **you will prosper. God blesses everyone who trusts him.** — *Proverbs 16:20 CEV*

10) **Don't be selfish and eager to get rich** — you will end up worse off than you can imagine. — *Proverbs 28:22 CEV*

11) **If we please God, he will make us wise, understanding, and happy. But if we sin, God will make us struggle for a living,** then he will give all we own to someone who pleases him. This makes no more sense than chasing the wind. — *Ecclesiastes 2:26 CEV*

12) **Give to others, and God will give to you.** Indeed, you will receive a full measure, a generous helping, poured into your hands — all that you can hold. **The measure you use for others is the one that God will use for you."** — *Luke 6:38 GNB*

13) I assure you, most solemnly I tell you, Unless a grain of wheat falls into the earth and dies, **it remains [just one grain; it never becomes more but lives] by itself alone.** But if it dies, it produces many others and yields a rich harvest. — *John 12:24 AMP*

14) My friends, we want you to know that the churches in Macedonia have shown others how kind God is. ²**Although they were going through hard times and were very poor, they were glad to give generously.** — *2 Corinthians 8:1-2 CEV*

15) [Remember] this: **he who sows sparingly** and **grudgingly will also reap sparingly** *and* **grudgingly,** and he who sows generously [that blessings may come to someone] will also **reap generously** *and* **with blessings.** — *2 Corinthians 9:6 AMP*

16) God gives seed to farmers and provides everyone with food. **He will increase what you have, so that you can give even more to those in need.** — *2 Corinthians 9:10 CEV*

17) **Don't get tired of helping others.** You will be **rewarded** when the time is right, **if you don't give up.** — *Galatians 6:9 CEV*

18) **We should help people whenever we can,** especially if they are followers of the Lord. — *Galatians 6:10 CEV*

19) I am not complaining about having too little. **I have learned to be satisfied with whatever I have.** — *Philippians 4:11 CEV*

20) I know what it is to be in need and what it is to have more than enough. I have learnt this secret, **so that anywhere, at any time, I am content, whether I am full or hungry, whether I have too much or too little.** — *Philippians 4:12 GNB*

21) I have strength for all things in Christ Who empowers me [I am ready for anything and equal to anything through Him Who infuses inner strength into me; I am self-sufficient in Christ's sufficiency]. — *Philippians 4:13 AMP*

22) It was good of you to help me when I was having such a hard time. — *Philippians 4:14 CEV*

23) I am not trying to get something from you, but I want you to receive the blessings that come from giving. — *Philippians 4:17 CEV*

24) I pray that God will take care of all your needs with the wonderful blessings that come from Christ Jesus! — *Philippians 4:19 CEV*

25) Instruct them to do as many good deeds as they can and to help everyone. Remind the rich to be generous and share what they have. — *1 Timothy 6:18 CEV*

5c) Conquering Your
Financial Struggles

Read On: January 29th | April 15th | July 1st | September 16th | December 2nd

1) You have obeyed me, and so you and your descendants will be a blessing to all nations on earth."
— *Genesis 22:18 CEV*

2) Remember that it is the LORD your God who gives you the power to become rich. He does this because he is still faithful today to the covenant that he made with your ancestors. — *Deuteronomy 8:18 GNB*

3) "If you obey the LORD your God and faithfully keep all his commands that I am giving you today, he will make you greater than any other nation on earth. — *Deuteronomy 28:1 GNB*

4) May the LORD answer you when you are in trouble! May the God of Jacob protect you! ²May he send you help from his Temple and give you aid from Mount Zion. ³May he accept all your offerings and be pleased with all your sacrifices. — *Psalm 20:1-3 GNB*

5) Do what the LORD wants, and he will give you your heart's desire.
— *Psalm 37:4 CEV*

6) Good people will prosper like palm trees, and they will grow strong like the cedars of Lebanon. — *Psalm 92:12*

7) Laziness leads to poverty; hard work makes you rich. — *Proverbs 10:4 CEV*

8) Anyone too lazy to cook will starve, but a hard worker is a valuable treasure.
— *Proverbs 12:27 CEV*

9) No matter how much you want, laziness won't help a bit, but hard work will reward you with more than enough.
— *Proverbs 13:4 CEV*

10) Hard work is worthwhile, but empty talk will make you poor.
— *Proverbs 14:23 CEV*

Scripture Therapy Daily Devotional For Men

11) **Work hard, and you will have a lot of food;** waste time, and you will have a lot of trouble. — *Proverbs 28:19 CEV*

12) **God blesses his loyal people,** but punishes all who want to get rich quick. — *Proverbs 28:20 CEV*

13) **If we please God, he will make us wise,** understanding, and happy. **But if we sin, God will make us struggle for a living,** then he will give all we own to someone who pleases him. This makes no more sense than chasing the wind. — *Ecclesiastes 2:26 CEV*

14) **Stay joined to me and let my teachings become part of you.** Then you can **pray** for **whatever you want,** and **your prayer will be answered.** — *John 15:7 CEV*

15) Since we are his children, **we will possess the blessings he keeps for his people, and we will also possess with Christ what God has kept for him; for if we share Christ's suffering, we will also share his glory.** — *Romans 8:17 GNB*

16) For, as the scripture says: **"The earth and everything in it belong to the Lord."** — *1 Corinthians 10:26 GNB*

17) As the scripture says, **"He gives generously to the needy; his kindness lasts forever."** — *2 Corinthians 9:9 GNB*

18) So if you belong to Christ, you are now part of Abraham's family, **and you will be given what God has promised.** — *Galatians 3:29 CEV*

19) **You cannot fool God,** so don't make a fool of yourself! You will harvest what you plant. ⁸**If you follow** your selfish desires, **you will harvest** destruction, **but if you follow** the Spirit, **you will harvest** eternal life. — *Galatians 6:7-8 CEV*

20) **I pray that God will take care of all your needs** with the wonderful blessings that come from **Christ Jesus!** — *Philippians 4:19 CEV*

21) But you must never stop looking at the perfect law that sets you free. **God will bless you in everything you do, if you listen and obey,** and don't just hear and forget. — *James 1:25 CEV*

5d) Having Enough Money to Meet Your Needs

Read On: January 30th | April 16th | July 2nd | September 17th | December 3rd

1) **Always let him lead you,** and he will **clear the road** for you to **follow.**
— *Proverbs 3:6 CEV*

2) Prize Wisdom highly and exalt her, **and she will exalt** *and* **promote you; she will bring you to honor** when you embrace her. — *Proverbs 4:8 AMP*

3) Being lazy will make you poor, but **hard work** will make you **rich.**
— *Proverbs 10:4 GNB*

4) When the Lord blesses you with riches, you have **nothing to regret.** — *Proverbs 10:22 CEV*

5) Work hard, and you will be a leader; be lazy, and you will end up a slave. — *Proverbs 12:24 CEV*

6) We make our own plans, **but the Lord decides where we will go.**
— *Proverbs 16:9 CEV*

7) Everything that happens in this world **happens at the time God chooses.**
— *Ecclesiastes 3:1 GNB*

8) Be generous, and someday **you will be rewarded.** — *Ecclesiastes 11:1 CEV*

9) If you worry about the weather **and don't plant seeds, you won't harvest a crop.**
— *Ecclesiastes 11:4 CEV*

10) Plant your seeds early in the morning and keep working in the field until dark. Who knows? Your work might pay off, **and your seeds might produce.**
— *Ecclesiastes 11:6 CEV*

11) Do not be afraid — I am with you! I am your God — let nothing terrify you! **I will make you strong and help you;** I will protect you and save you.
— *Isaiah 41:10 GNB*

12) "Yes," said Jesus, "if you yourself can! **Everything is possible for the person who has faith."**
—*Mark 9:23 GNB*

84

13) **Give to others, and God will give to you.** Indeed, you will receive a full measure, a generous helping, poured into your hands — all that you can hold. **The measure you use for others is the one that God will use for you."** — *Luke 6:38 GNB*

14) Jesus said to her, Did I not tell you *and* promise you **that if you would believe** *and* **rely on Me, you would see the glory of God?** — *John 11:40 AMP*

15) **There is a real opportunity here** for great and worthwhile work, even though **there are many opponents.** — *1 Corinthians 16:9 GNB*

17) Remember **that the person who sows few seeds will have a small crop;** the one **who sows many seeds will have a large crop.** ⁷You should each give, then, as you have decided, **not with regret or out of a sense of duty;** for God loves the one who gives gladly. — *2 Corinthians 9:6-7 GNB*

16) We are often troubled, **but not crushed;** sometimes in doubt, **but never in despair.** — *2 Corinthians 4:8 GNB*

18) And God is able to give you **more than you need,** so that you will always have all you need for yourselves and more than enough **for every good cause.** — *2 Corinthians 9:8 GNB*

19) To him who by means of **his power working in us is able to do so much more than we can ever ask for, or even think of:** — *Ephesians 3:20 GNB*

20) **Don't worry about anything, but pray about everything.** With thankful hearts offer up your **prayers** and **requests** to **God.** — *Philippians 4:6 CEV*

21) **I have the strength to face all conditions** by the power that **Christ** gives me. — *Philippians 4:13 GNB*

22) I know what you do; I know that you have a little power; **you have followed my teaching and have been faithful to me. I have opened a door in front of you, which no one can close.** — *Revelation 3:8 GNB*

5e) Conquering Poverty and Lack

Read On: January 31st | April 17th | July 3rd | September 18th | December 4th

1) So then, you must never think that you have made yourselves wealthy **by your own power and strength.**
— *Deuteronomy 8:17 GNB*

2) Remember that it is the LORD your God who gives you the power to become rich. He does this because he is **still faithful** today to the covenant that he made with your ancestors. — *Deuteronomy 8:18 GNB*

3) But Jabez prayed to the God of Israel, **"Bless me, God, and give me much land. Be with me and keep me from anything evil that might cause me pain."** And God gave him what he prayed for. — *1 Chronicles 4:10 GNB*

4) You have changed my sadness into a joyful dance; you have taken away my sorrow and surrounded me with joy.
— *Psalm 30:11 GNB*

5) I thank you from my heart, and I will never stop singing your praises, my LORD and my God. — *Psalm 30:12 CEV*

6) Be generous, and you will be prosperous. Help others, and you **will be helped.**
— *Proverbs 11:25 GNB*

7) When you give to the poor, it is like lending to the LORD, **and the LORD will pay you back.** — *Proverbs 19:17 GNB*

8) Some people **are too lazy to lift a hand to feed themselves.**
— *Proverbs 19:24 CEV*

9) If you are too lazy to plow, **don't expect a harvest.**
— *Proverbs 20:4 CEV*

10) If you **sleep all the time,** you will starve; **if you get up and work, you will have enough food.** — *Proverbs 20:13 CEV*

11) Giving to the poor will keep you from poverty, but if you close your eyes to their needs, everyone will curse you. — *Proverbs 28:27 CEV*

12) God is my saviour; I will trust him and not be afraid. The LORD gives me **power** and **strength;** he is my saviour. — *Isaiah 12:2 GNB*

Scripture Therapy Daily Devotional For Men

13) **Make the tent you live in larger; lengthen its ropes and strengthen the pegs!** — *Isaiah 54:2 GNB*

14) And Jesus, replying, said to them, **Have faith in God [constantly].** — *Mark 11:22 AMP*

15) **If you have faith in God and don't doubt,** you can tell this mountain to get up and jump into the sea, **and it will.** — *Mark 11:23 CEV*

17) My little group of disciples, don't be afraid! **Your Father wants to give you the kingdom.** — *Luke 12:32 CEV*

19) What you are doing is much more than a service that supplies God's people with what they need. **It is something that will make many others thank God.** ¹³The way in which you have proved yourselves by this service **will bring honour and praise to God.** You believed the message about Christ, and **you obeyed it by sharing generously with God's people and with everyone else.** — *2 Corinthians 9:12-15 CEV*

16) For this reason I am telling you, **whatever** you ask for in prayer, **believe (trust and be confident) that it is granted to you, and you will [get it].** — *Mark 11:24 AMP*

18) **Who made you superior to others? Didn't God give you everything you have?** Well, then, how can you boast, as if what you have were not **a gift?** — *1 Corinthians 4:7 GNB*

20) **And my God will liberally supply (fill to the full) your every need** according to His riches in glory in Christ Jesus. — *Philippians 4:19 AMP*

21) Now, God has offered us the promise that we may receive that rest he spoke about. **Let us take care, then, that none of you will be found to have failed to receive that promised rest.** — *Hebrews 4:1 GNB*

22) If any of you need wisdom, **you should ask God, and it will be given to you. God is generous and won't correct you for asking** — *James 1:5 CEV*

23) **But when you pray, you must believe and not doubt at all.** Whoever doubts is like a wave in the sea that is driven and blown about by the wind. — *James 1:6 GNB*

24) **People like that, unable to make up their minds and undecided in all they do,** must not think that they will receive anything from the Lord.
— *James 1:7-8 GNB*

CHAPTER 6

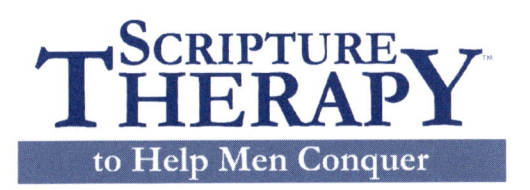

SCRIPTURE THERAPY™
to Help Men Conquer
HEALTH ISSUES

TOPICS

6a) Staying Strong and Healthy
Read On: February 1st | April 18th | July 4th | September 19th | December 5th

6b) God's Protection Over Your Life
Read On: February 2nd | April 19th | July 5th | September 20th | December 6th

6c) Protection From Harm or Danger
Read On: February 3rd | April 20th | July 6th | September 21st | December 7th

6d) Healing From Sickness and Disease
Read On: February 4th | April 21st | July 7th | September 22nd | December 8th

6e) Staying Mentally and Emotionally Healthy
Read On: February 5th | April 22nd | July 8th | September 23rd | December 9th

6f) The Lord's Protection From Illness and Disease
Read On: February 6th | April 23rd | July 9th | September 24th | December 10th

6a) Staying
Strong and Healthy

Read On: February 1st | April 18th | July 4th | September 19th | December 5th

1) He forgives all my sins and **heals all my diseases.** — *Psalm 103:3 GNB*

2) He keeps me from the grave and blesses me with love and mercy. — *Psalm 103:4 GNB*

3) He fills my life **with good things, so that I stay young and strong like an eagle.** — *Psalm 103:5 GNB*

4) By the power of his own word, **he healed you and saved you from destruction.** — *Psalm 107:20 CEV*

5) God sees that justice is done, **and he watches over everyone who is faithful to him.** — *Proverbs 2:8 CEV*

6) I have taught you **wisdom and the right way to live.** ¹²Nothing will stand in your way **if you walk wisely, and you will not stumble** when you run. — *Proverbs 4:11-12 GNB*

7) My child, **listen carefully to everything I say.** ²¹Don't forget a single word, but think about it all. ²²**Knowing these teachings will mean true life and good health for you.** — *Proverbs 4:20-22 CEV*

8) Sharp words cut like a sword, **but words of wisdom heal.** — *Proverbs 12:18 CEV*

9) Kind words are good medicine, but deceitful words **can really hurt.** — *Proverbs 15:4 CEV*

10) A friendly smile makes you happy, and **good news** makes you **feel strong.** — *Proverbs 15:30 CEV*

11) He was wounded and crushed because of our sins; by taking our punishment, **he made us completely well.** — *Isaiah 53:5 CEV*

12) The LORD will always guide you and provide good things to eat when you are in the desert. He will make you healthy. You will be like a garden that has plenty of water or like a stream that never runs dry. — *Isaiah 58:11 CEV*

13) **And I will always guide you and satisfy you with good things.** I will keep you strong and well. You will be like a garden that has plenty of water, like a spring of water that never runs dry.
— *Isaiah 58:11 GNB*

14) If the Spirit of God, who raised Jesus from death, lives in you, then he who raised Christ from death **will also give life to your mortal bodies by the presence of his Spirit in you.**
— *Romans 8:11 GNB*

15) Don't you know that your body is the temple of the Holy Spirit, **who lives in you** and who was given to you by God? You do not belong to yourselves but to God.
— *1 Corinthians 6:19 GNB*

16) God paid a great price for you. **So use your body to honour God.**
— *1 Corinthians 6:20 CEV*

17) If you have faith when you pray for sick people, they will get well. The Lord will heal them, and if they have sinned, he will forgive them.
— *James 5:15 CEV*

18) Christ carried the burden of our sins. He was nailed to the cross, so that we would stop sinning and start living right. **By his cuts and bruises you are healed.** — *1 Peter 2:24 CEV*

19) My dear friend, I **pray that everything may go well with you** and that you may be in good health - as I know you are well in spirit.
— *3 John 1:2 GNB*

20) Then it flowed down the middle of the city's main street. On each side of the river **are trees that grow a different kind of fruit each month of the year. The fruit gives life, and the leaves are used as medicine to heal the nations.** — *Revelation 22:2 CEV*

6b) God's
Protection Over Your Life

Read On: February 2nd | April 19th | July 5th | September 20th | December 6th

1) So then, **you must never think** that you have made yourselves wealthy **by your own power and strength.** — *Deuteronomy 8:17 GNB*

2) Remember that it is the LORD your God who gives **you the power to become rich.** He does this because he is **still faithful** today to the covenant that he made with your ancestors. — *Deuteronomy 8:18 GNB*

4) You have changed my sadness into a joyful dance; you have taken away my sorrow and surrounded me with joy. —*Psalm 30:11 GNB*

5) **I thank you from my heart,** and **I will never stop singing your praises,** my LORD and my God. — *Psalm 30:12 CEV*

3) But Jabez prayed to the God of Israel, "Bless me, God, and give me much land. Be with me and keep me from anything evil that might cause me pain." And God gave him what he prayed for. — *1 Chronicles 4:10 GNB*

6) **Be generous, and you will be prosperous.** Help others, and you **will be helped.** — *Proverbs 11:25 GNB*

7) He who dwells in the secret place of the Most High **shall remain stable** *and* **fixed** under the shadow of the Almighty [Whose power no foe can withstand]. — *Psalm 91:1 AMP*

8) He will cover you with his wings; you will be safe in his care; his faithfulness **will protect and defend you.** — *Psalm 91:4 GNB*

9) **You need not fear any dangers at night** or sudden attacks during the day. — *Psalm 91:5 GNB*

10) You have made **the Lord your defender, the Most High your protector,** ¹⁰and so **no disaster will strike you, no violence will come near your home.** — *Psalm 91:9-10 GNB*

Scripture Therapy Daily Devotional For Men

11) God will put his angels in charge of you to protect you wherever you go. — *Psalm 91:11 GNB*

12) God says, "I will save those who love me and will protect those who acknowledge me as Lord. — *Psalm 91:14 GNB*

13) When you are in trouble, call out to me. I will answer and be there to protect and honour you. — *Psalm 91:15 CEV*

14) I will reward them with long life; I will save them." — *Psalm 91:16 GNB*

15) By the power of his own word, he healed you and saved you from destruction. — *Psalm 107:20 CEV*

16) As long as you obey his commands, you are safe, and a wise person knows how and when to do it. — *Ecclesiastes 8:5 GNB*

17) I will bless you with a future filled with hope — a future of success, not of suffering. — *Jeremiah 29:11 CEV*

18) But not a hair of your head shall perish. — *Luke 21:18 AMP*

19) A thief comes only to rob, kill, and destroy. I came so that everyone would have life, and have it fully. — *John 10:10 CEV*

20) Put on all the armour that God gives you, so that you will be able to stand up against the Devil's evil tricks. — *Ephesians 6:11 GNB*

21) So put on God's armour now! Then when the evil day comes, you will be able to resist the enemy's attacks; and after fighting to the end, you will still hold your ground. — *Ephesians 6:13 GNB*

22) Don't worry about anything, but pray about everything. With thankful hearts offer up your prayers and requests to God. — *Philippians 4:6 CEV*

23) I have the strength to face all conditions by the power that Christ gives me. — *Philippians 4:13 GNB*

6c) Protection From
Harm or Danger

Read On: February 3rd | April 20th | July 6th | September 21st | December 7th

1) I lie down and sleep, and **all night long** the LORD **protects me.**
— *Psalm 3:5 GNB*

2) I can lie down and **sleep soundly** because **you,** LORD, **will keep me safe.**
— *Psalm 4:8 CEV*

3) The LORD will keep you safe from secret traps and **deadly diseases.** — *Psalm 91:3 CEV*

4) The LORD will guard you; he is by your side **to protect you.** — *Psalm 121:5 GNB*

5) The LORD will protect you and keep you safe from all **dangers.** — *Psalm 121:7 CEV*

6) The LORD will protect you now and always **wherever you go.** — *Psalm 121:8 CEV*

7) He protects those who treat others fairly, and guards those who are **devoted** to him. — *Proverbs 2:8 GNB*

8) You will walk safely and never stumble. — *Proverbs 3:23 CEV*

9) You will not be afraid when you go to bed, and you will sleep soundly through the night. — *Proverbs 3:24 GNB*

10) You can be sure that **the** LORD **will protect you from harm.**
— *Proverbs 3:26 CEV*

11) I am Wisdom. If you follow me, **you will live a long time.**
— *Proverbs 9:11 CEV*

12) Keep what you know to yourself, **and you will be safe;** talk too much, and you are done for. — *Proverbs 13:3 CEV*

13) The LORD is a mighty tower where his people can run for safety. — *Proverbs 18:10 CEV*

Scripture Therapy Daily Devotional For Men

14) **You, LORD, give perfect peace** to those who keep their **purpose firm and put their trust in you.** — *Isaiah 26:3 GNB*

15) I am the LORD your **God.** **I am holding your hand,** so don't be afraid. **I am here to help you.** — *Isaiah 41:13 CEV*

16) Israel, the LORD who created you says, **"Do not be afraid — I will save you.** I have called you by name **— you are mine.** — *Isaiah 43:1 GNB*

17) When you pass through deep waters, **I will be with you; your troubles will not overwhelm you.** When you pass through fire, **you will not be burnt; the hard trials that come will not hurt you.** — *Isaiah 43:2 GNB*

18) At that time I will make a covenant with all the wild animals and birds, **so that they will not harm my people.** I will also remove all weapons of war from the land, all swords and bows, **and will let my people live in peace and safety.** — *Hosea 2:18 GNB*

19) They will pick up serpents; and [even] if they drink anything deadly, **it will not hurt them; they will lay their hands on the sick, and they will get well.** — *Mark 16:18 AMP*

20) I have given you the power to trample on snakes and scorpions **and to defeat the power of your enemy Satan. Nothing can harm you.** — *Luke 10:19 CEV*

21) But not a hair of your head shall perish. — *Luke 21:18 AMP*

22) And God's peace, which is far beyond human understanding, **will keep your hearts and minds safe in union with Christ Jesus.** — *Philippians 4:7 GNB*

23) The Lord will always keep me from being harmed by evil, and he will bring me safely into his heavenly kingdom. Praise him for ever and ever! Amen. — *2 Timothy 4:18 CEV*

6d) Healing From
Sickness and Disease

Read On: February 4th | April 21st | July 7th | September 22nd | December 8th

1) You will no longer suffer with the same horrible diseases that you sometimes had in Egypt. You will be healthy, but the Lord will make your enemies suffer from those diseases. — *Deuteronomy 7:15 CEV*

2) I prayed to you, Lord God, and you healed me. — *Psalm 30:2 CEV*

3) Trust the Lord and live right! The land will be yours, and you will be safe. [4]Do what the Lord wants, and he will give you your heart's desire. [5]Let the Lord lead you and trust him to help. — *Psalm 37:3-5 CEV*

4) Don't give in to worry or anger; it only leads to trouble. — *Psalm 37:8 GNB*

5) The LORD forgives our sins, heals us when we are sick, [4]and protects us from death. His kindness and love are a crown on our heads. [5]Each day that we live, he provides for our needs and gives us the strength of a young eagle. — *Psalm 103:3-5 CEV*

6) He keeps me from the grave and blesses me with love and mercy. — *Psalm 103:4 GNB*

7) He fills my life with good things, so that I stay young and strong like an eagle. — *Psalm 103:5 GNB*

8) He healed them with his command and saved them from the grave. — *Psalm 107:20 GNB*

9) He renews our hopes and heals our bodies. — *Psalm 147:3 CEV*

10) Your words and your deeds bring life to everyone, including me. Please make me healthy and strong again. — *Isaiah 38:16 CEV*

11) But because of our sins he was wounded, beaten because of the evil we did. We are healed by the punishment he suffered, made whole by the blows he received. — *Isaiah 53:5 GNB*

14) If the Spirit of God, who raised Jesus from death, **lives in you,** then he who raised Christ from death **will also give life to your mortal bodies by the presence of his Spirit in you.** — *Romans 8:11 GNB*

12) You, LORD, are the one I praise. **So heal me and rescue me! Then I will be completely well and perfectly safe.** — *Jeremiah 17:14 CEV*

13) Show your mighty power, **as we heal people and perform miracles and wonders** in the name of your holy Servant Jesus. — *Acts 4:30 CEV*

16) To him who **by means of his power working in us** is able to do so much more **than we can ever ask** for, or even think of. — *Ephesians 3:20 GNB*

15) But thanks be to God, **Who gives us the victory [making us conquerors]** through our Lord **Jesus Christ.** — *1 Corinthians 15:57 AMP*

18) So put on God's armour now! Then when the evil day comes, you **will be able to resist the enemy's attacks;** and after fighting to the end, **you will still hold your ground.** — *Ephesians 6:13 GNB*

17) In conclusion, be strong in the Lord [be empowered through your union with Him]; draw your strength from Him [that strength which His boundless might provides]. — *Ephesians 6:10 AMP*

20) He rescued us from the **power of darkness** and brought us safe into the kingdom of his dear Son. — *Colossians 1:13 GNB*

21) Let us have confidence, then, and approach God's throne, where there is grace. There we will receive mercy and **find grace to help us** just when we need it. — *Hebrews 4:16 GNB*

19) At all times carry faith as a shield; for with it you will be able to put out all the burning arrows shot by the Evil One. — *Ephesians 6:16 GNB*

22) And the prayer [that is] of faith will save him who is sick, and the Lord will restore him; and if he has committed sins, he will be forgiven.
— *James 5:15 AMP*

23) My dear friend, **I pray that everything may go well with you** and that **you may be in good health** - as I know you are well in spirit.
— *3 John 1:2 GNB*

6e) Staying Mentally and Emotionally Healthy

Read On: February 5th | April 22nd | July 8th | September 23rd | December 9th

1) Moses told the people, **Fear not; stand still** (firm, confident, undismayed) **and see the salvation of the Lord which He will work for you today.** For the Egyptians you have seen today you shall never see again. ¹⁴**The LORD will fight for you, and you shall hold your peace and remain at rest.** — *Exodus 14:13-14 AMP*

2) The LORD is my light and my salvation; I will fear no one. **The LORD protects me from all danger; I will never be afraid.** — *Psalm 27:1 GNB*

3) The LORD is there **to rescue all who are discouraged and have given up hope.** — *Psalm 34:18 CEV*

4) The LORD's people may suffer a lot, **but he will always bring them safely through.** — *Psalm 34:19 CEV*

5) Rescue me from cruel and violent enemies, LORD! — *Psalm 140:1 CEV*

6) Being cheerful keeps you healthy. **It is slow death to be gloomy** all the time. — *Proverbs 17:22 GNB*

7) Do not be afraid — I am with you! I am your God — **let nothing terrify you!** I will make you strong and help you; I will protect you and save you. — *Isaiah 41:10 GNB*

8) Jesus turned. He saw the woman and said, **"Don't worry! You are now well because of your faith."** At that moment she was healed. — *Matthew 9:22 CEV*

9) Jesus told him, "You may go. **Your eyes are healed because of your faith."** Straight away the man could see, and he went down the road with Jesus. — *Mark 10:52 CEV*

10) When Jesus heard this, he told Jairus, **"Don't worry! Have faith, and your daughter will get well."** — *Luke 8:50 CEV*

Scripture Therapy Daily Devotional For Men

11) You see this man, and you know him. **He put his faith in the name of Jesus and was made strong. Faith in Jesus made this man completely well** while everyone was watching. — *Acts 3:16 CEV*

12) "When that day comes, you will not ask me for anything. I am telling you the truth: **the Father will give you whatever you ask of him for in my name.** ²⁴Until now you have not asked for anything in my name; **ask and you will receive, so that your happiness may be complete.** — *John 16:23-24 GNB*

13) We often suffer, but we are never crushed. **Even when we don't know what to do, we never give up.** ⁹In times of trouble, **God is with us,** and when we are knocked down, **we get up again.** — *2 Corinthians 4:8-9 CEV*

14) But I reckon my own life to be worth nothing to me; **I only want to complete my mission and finish the work that the Lord Jesus gave me to do,** which is to declare the Good News about the grace of God. — *Acts 20:24 GNB*

15) Stop being bitter and angry with others. Don't yell at one another or curse each other or ever be rude. — *Ephesians 4:31 CEV*

16) We never give up. Our bodies are gradually dying, but we ourselves are being made stronger each day. — *2 Corinthians 4:16 CEV*

17) So let's come near God with pure hearts and a confidence that comes from having faith. Let's keep our hearts pure, our consciences free from evil, and our bodies washed with clean water. — *Hebrews 10:22 CEV*

18) And this small and temporary trouble we suffer **will bring us a tremendous and eternal glory, much greater than the trouble.** — *2 Corinthians 4:17 GNB*

19) Such a large crowd of witnesses is all around us! **So we must get rid of everything that slows us down, especially the sin that just won't let go. And we must be determined to run the race** that is ahead of us. — *Hebrews 12:1 CEV*

20) Casting the whole of your care [all your anxieties, all your worries, all your concerns, once and for all] on Him, for He cares for you affectionately and cares about you watchfully. — *1 Peter 5:7 AMP*

100

6f) The Lord's Protection From
Illness and Disease

Read On: February 6th | April 23rd | July 9th | September 24th | December 10th

1) In times of trouble, **you will protect me.** You will **hide me** in your tent **and keep me safe** on top of a mighty rock. — *Psalm 27:5 CEV*

2) When his people pray for help, **he listens and rescues them from their troubles.** — *Psalm 34:17 CEV*

3) the LORD preserves them completely; not one of their bones is broken. — *Psalm 34:20 GNB*

4) God is our shelter and strength, always ready to help in times of trouble. — *Psalm 46:1 GNB*

5) Whoever goes to the LORD for safety, whoever remains under the protection of the Almighty, ²can say to him, "You are my defender and protector. **You are my God; in you I trust."** — *Psalm 91:1-2 GNB*

6) He will keep you safe from all hidden dangers and from all **deadly diseases.** — *Psalm 91:3 GNB*

7) He will cover you with his wings; you will be safe in his care; his faithfulness will **protect** and **defend** you. — *Psalm 91:4 GNB*

8) You need not fear any dangers at night or sudden attacks during the day ⁶or the plagues that strike in the dark **or the evils that kill in daylight.** — *Psalm 91:5-6 GNB*

9) You will not be harmed, though thousands fall **all around you.** — *Psalm 91:7 CEV*

10) You have made the LORD your defender, the Most High your protector, ¹⁰and so **no disaster will strike you, no violence will come near your home.** — *Psalm 91:9-10 GNB*

101

11) God will put his angels in charge of you to protect you wherever you go. ¹²They will hold you up with their hands to keep you from hurting your feet on the stones. — *Psalm 91:11-12 GNB*

12) God says, "I will save those who love me and will protect those who acknowledge me as LORD — *Psalm 91:14 GNB*

13) When you are in trouble, call out to me. I will answer and be there to protect and honour you. ¹⁶You will live a long life and see my saving power." — *Psalm 91:15-16 CEV*

14) Keep me alive, so I can praise you, and let me find help in your teachings. — *Psalm 119:175 CEV*

15) Respect and serve the LORD! Your reward will be wealth, a long life, and honour. — *Proverbs 22:4 CEV*

16) But those who wait for the Lord [who expect, look for, and hope in Him] shall change and renew their strength and power; they shall lift their wings and mount up [close to God] as eagles [mount up to the sun]; they shall run and not be weary, they shall walk and not faint or become tired. — *Isaiah 40:31 AMP*

17) Jesus answered, "The Scriptures say: 'No one can live only on food. People need every word that God has spoken.'" — *Matthew 4:4 CEV*

18) God loved the people of this world so much that he gave his only Son, so that everyone who has faith in him will have eternal life and never really die. — *John 3:16 CEV*

19) I give you peace, the kind of peace that only I can give. It isn't like the peace that this world can give. So don't be worried or afraid. — *John 14:27 CEV*

CHAPTER 7

Scripture Therapy™ to Help Men Conquer Success Issues

TOPICS

7a) Conquering The Fears Limiting Your Potential
Read On: February 7th | April 24th | July 10th | September 25th | December 11th

7b) The Lord's Guidance to Help You Succeed
Read On: February 8th | April 25th | July 11th | September 26th | December 12th

7c) Conquering Barriers to Your Success
Read On: February 9th | April 26th | July 12th | September 27th | December 13th

7d) Determination to Persevere Through Challenges
Read On: February 10th | April 27th | July 13th | September 28th | December 14th

7e) Conquering The Challenges You Face in Life
Read On: February 11th | April 28th | July 14th | September 29th | December 15th

7f) Belief in God's Covenant Promise to Bless You
Read On: February 12th | April 29th | July 15th | September 30th | December 16th

7g) Inspiration to Conquer Your Fears and Doubts
Read On: February 13th | April 30th | July 16th | October 1st | December 17th

7h) Your Motivation to Work Hard and Succeed
Read On: February 14th | May 1st | July 17th | October 2nd | December 18th

7i) Self-Belief to Succeed in Everything You Do
Read On: February 15th | May 2nd | July 18th | October 3rd | December 19th

7j) Confidence in God to Provide for Your Needs
Read On: February 16th | May 3rd | July 19th | October 4th | December 20th

7k) Your Confidence and Determination to Succeed
Read On: February 17th | May 4th | July 20th | October 5th | December 21st

7a) Conquering The Fears Limiting
Your Potential

Read On: February 7th | April 24th | July 10th | September 25th | December 11th

1) **Remember that I have commanded you to be determined and confident! Don't be afraid or discouraged, for I, the L**ORD **your God, am with you wherever you go."** — *Joshua 1:9 GNB*

2) Trust in the LORD. **Have faith,** do not despair. **Trust in the L**ORD**.** — *Psalm 27:14 GNB*

3) I prayed to the LORD, **and he** answered me; **he freed me from all my fears.** — *Psalm 34:4 GNB*

4) When I am afraid, O LORD Almighty, **I put my trust in you.** — *Psalm 56:3 GNB*

5) I trust in God and am not afraid; I praise him for what he has promised. **What can a mere human being do to me?** — *Psalm 56:4 GNB*

6) Wicked people run away when no one chases them, **but those who live right are as brave as lions.** — *Proverbs 28:1 CEV*

7) Do not be afraid — I am with you! I am your God — let nothing terrify you! **I will make you strong and help you;** I will protect you and save you. — *Isaiah 41:10 GNB*

8) But no weapon that is formed against you shall prosper, and every tongue that shall rise against you in judgment you shall show to be in the wrong. This [peace, righteousness, security, triumph over opposition] is the heritage of the servants of the Lord [those in whom the ideal Servant of the Lord is reproduced]; this is the righteousness or the vindication which they obtain from Me [this is that which I impart to them as their justification], says the Lord. — *Isaiah 54:17 AMP*

9) Do not be afraid of them, for I will be with you to protect you. I, the LORD, have spoken!" — *Jeremiah 1:8 GNB*

10) "Call to me, and I will answer you; I will tell you wonderful and marvelous things that you know nothing about. — *Jeremiah 33:3 GNB*

Scripture Therapy Daily Devotional For Men

11) For this reason I am telling you, whatever you ask for in prayer, **believe (trust and be confident) that it is granted to you, and you will [get it].** — *Mark 11:24 AMP*

12) For with God nothing is ever impossible and no word from God shall be without power or impossible of fulfillment. — *Luke 1:37 AMP*

13) "Do not be worried and upset," Jesus told them. **"Believe in God** and believe also in me. — *John 14:1 GNB*

14) Peace I leave with you; My [own] peace I now give *and* bequeath to you. Not as the world gives do I give to you. Do not let your hearts be troubled, neither let them be afraid. **[Stop allowing yourselves to be agitated and disturbed; and do not permit yourselves to be fearful and intimidated and cowardly and unsettled.]** — *John 14:27 AMP*

15) The weapons we use in our fight are not the world's weapons **but God's powerful weapons, which we use to destroy strongholds. We destroy false arguments.** — *2 Corinthians 10:4 GNB*

16) I have not yet reached my goal, and I am not perfect. **But Christ has taken hold of me. So I keep on running and struggling to take hold of the prize.** — *Philippians 3:12 CEV*

17) My friends, I don't feel that I have already arrived. **But I forget what is behind, and I struggle for what is ahead.** — *Philippians 3:13 CEV*

18) I run towards the goal, so that I can win the prize of being called to heaven. This is the prize that God offers because of what Christ Jesus has done. — *Philippians 3:14 CEV*

19) Do not fret *or* **have any anxiety about anything,** but in every circumstance and in everything, by prayer and petition **(definite requests), with thanksgiving, continue to make your wants known to God.** — *Philippians 4:6 AMP*

20) Christ gives me the strength to face anything. — *Philippians 4:13 CEV*

21) Use the gift you were given when the prophets spoke and the group of church leaders blessed you by placing their hands on you. — *1 Timothy 4:14 CEV*

105

7b) The Lord's Guidance to Help You
Succeed

Read On: February 8th | April 25th | July 11th | September 26h | December 12th

1) No man shall be able to stand before you all the days of your life. As I was with Moses, **so I will be with you; I will not fail you** or forsake you. — *Joshua 1:5 AMP*

2) You will show me the path that leads to life; your presence fills me with **joy and brings me pleasure forever.** — *Psalm 16:11 GNB*

3) He gives me new strength. **He guides me in the right paths,** as he has promised. — *Psalm 23:3 GNB*

4) I [the Lord] will instruct you and teach you in the way you should go; I will **counsel** you with My eye upon you. — *Psalm 32:8 AMP*

5) Give yourself to the LORD; trust in him, and **he will help you.** — *Psalm 37:5 GNB*

6) Your word is a lamp to guide me and a **light** for my path. — *Psalm 119:105 GNB*

7) Here are proverbs that will help you recognize wisdom and good advice, and understand sayings with deep meaning. ³They can teach you how to live intelligently and how to be honest, just, and fair. — *Proverbs 1:2-3 GNB*

8) They can make an inexperienced person **clever** and **teach young people how to be resourceful.** ⁵These proverbs can even **add to the knowledge** of the wise and give **guidance** to the educated. — *Proverbs 1:4-5 GNB*

9) Listen to what is wise and try to **understand** it. — *Proverbs 2:2 GNB*

10) God gives helpful advice to everyone who obeys him and **protects** all of those who live as they should. — *Proverbs 2:7 CEV*

11) My child, remember my teachings and instructions and obey them completely. ²They will **help** you live a **long** and **prosperous** life. — *Proverbs 3:1-2 CEV*

12) With all your heart **you must trust the LORD and not your own judgment.** — *Proverbs 3:5 CEV*

13) Always let him lead you, and he will **clear the road** for you to **follow.** — *Proverbs 3:6 CEV*

14) But the path of the [uncompromisingly] just *and* **righteous** is like the light of dawn, **that shines more and more** (brighter and clearer) until **[it reaches its full strength and glory in]** the perfect day [to be prepared]. — *Proverbs 4:18 AMP*

15) Pay attention to what I say, my son. **Listen** to my words. — *Proverbs 4:20 GNB*

16) Without good advice everything goes wrong — it takes **careful planning** for things to go **right.** — *Proverbs 15:22 CEV*

17) Share your plans with the LORD, and you will **succeed.** — *Proverbs 16:3 CEV*

18) Roll your works upon the Lord [commit and trust them wholly to Him; He will cause your thoughts to become agreeable to His will, and] so shall your **plans** be **established** and **succeed.** — *Proverbs 16:3 AMP*

19) You may make your plans, **but God directs your actions.** — *Proverbs 16:9 GNB*

20) As long as you obey his commands, you are safe, and a wise person knows **how** and **when** to do it. — *Ecclesiastes 8:5 GNB*

21) "I myself will prepare your way, leveling mountains and **hills.** I will break down **bronze gates** and **smash** their **iron bars.** — *Isaiah 45:2 GNB*

22) Make good use of **every opportunity you have,** because these are evil days. — *Ephesians 5:16 GNB*

23) But if any of you lack wisdom, you should pray to God, who will give it to you; because **God gives generously** and graciously to all. — *James 1:5 GNB*

24) But when you **ask for something, you must have faith and not doubt. Anyone who doubts** is like an ocean wave tossed around in a storm. — *James 1:6 CEV*

7c) Conquering
Barriers to Your Success

Read On: February 9th | April 26th | July 12th | September 27th | December 13th

1) So give me the **wisdom I need to rule your people** with justice and to know **the difference** between **good** and **evil.** Otherwise, how would I ever be able to rule this great people of yours?" — *1 Kings 3:9 GNB*

2) I **gain wisdom from your laws,** and so I hate all bad conduct. — *Psalm 119:104 GNB*

3) Yes, **beg for knowledge; plead for insight.** — *Proverbs 2:3 GNB*

4) It is the **LORD** who gives wisdom; from him come knowledge and understanding. — *Proverbs 2:6 GNB*

5) Wisdom offers you long life, as well as wealth and honour. — *Proverbs 3:16 GNB*

6) If you **love Wisdom** and don't **reject her,** she will **watch over you.** — *Proverbs 4:6 CEV*

7) Getting wisdom is the most important thing you can do. Whatever else you get, get insight. — *Proverbs 4:7 GNB*

8) Prize Wisdom highly and **exalt her,** and **she will exalt** and **promote you;** she will bring you to **honor** when you **embrace her.** — *Proverbs 4:8 AMP*

9) Do yourself a favour **by having good sense** — you will be glad you did. — *Proverbs 19:8 CEV*

10) If you want to **stay out of trouble, be careful what you say.** — *Proverbs 21:23 GNB*

11) Show me someone who does a good job, and I will show you someone who is **better than most** and **worthy of the company of kings.** — *Proverbs 22:29 GNB*

12) If you don't sharpen your axe, it will be harder to use; if you are clever, you'll know what to do. — *Ecclesiastes 10:10 CEV*

13) You are the light of the world. A city set on a hill cannot be hidden. — *Matthew 5:14 AMP*

14) Let your light so shine before men that they may see your **moral excellence** *and* your praiseworthy, noble, and **good deeds** and recognize **and** honor **and praise and glorify** your Father Who is in heaven. — *Matthew 5:16 AMP*

15) But God has brought you into union with Christ Jesus, and God has made Christ to be our wisdom. **By him we are put right with God; we become God's holy people and are set free.** — *1 Corinthians 1:30 GNB*

16) Act like people with good sense and not like fools. ¹⁶These are evil times, **so make every minute count.** ¹⁷Don't be stupid. **Instead, find out what the Lord wants you to do.** — *Ephesians 5:15-17 CEV*

17) We have not stopped praying for you since the first day we heard about you. In fact, **we always pray that God will show you everything he wants you to do** and that **you may have all the wisdom and understanding** that his **Spirit** gives. — *Colossians 1:9 CEV*

18) That you may walk **(live and conduct yourselves) in a manner worthy of the Lord, fully pleasing to Him** *and* desiring to please Him in all things, bearing **fruit** in every **good work** and **steadily growing** *and* increasing in and by the knowledge of **God** [with fuller, deeper, and clearer insight, acquaintance, and recognition]. — *Colossians 1:10 AMP*

19) He is the **key** that **opens** all the **hidden treasures** of **God's wisdom** and **knowledge.** — *Colossians 2:3 GNB*

20) If any of you is deficient in wisdom, let him **ask of the giving God** [Who gives] to everyone liberally and ungrudgingly, without reproaching or faultfinding, **and it will be given him.** — *James 1:5 AMP*

21) Do not deceive yourselves by just **listening to his word;** instead, **put it into practice.**
— *James 1:22 GNB*

22) Are any of you wise or sensible? **Then show it by living right** and by **being humble** and wise **in everything you do.**
— *James 3:13 CEV*

23) Yet even when you do pray, your prayers are not answered, **because you pray just for selfish reasons.** — *James 4:3 CEV*

7d) Determination to Persevere Through Challenges

Read On: February 10th | April 27th | July 13th | September 28th | December 14th

1) Moses told the people, **Fear not; stand still (firm, confident, undismayed) and see the salvation of the Lord which** He will work for you today. For the Egyptians you have seen today you shall never see again. **¹⁴The Lord will fight for you, and you shall hold your peace** *and* **remain at rest.** — *Exodus 14:13-14 AMP*

2) If you worry about the weather and don't plant seeds, you won't harvest a crop. — *Ecclesiastes 11:4 CEV*

3) Do not be afraid — **I am with you! I am your God — let nothing terrify you!** I will make you strong and help you; **I will protect you and save you.** — *Isaiah 41:10 GNB*

4) And from the days of John the Baptist until the present time, the kingdom of heaven has endured violent assault, and violent men **seize it by force [as a precious prize — a share in the heavenly kingdom is sought with most ardent zeal and intense exertion].** — *Matthew 11:12 AMP*

5) The apostles said to the Lord, **"Make our faith greater."** — *Luke 17:5 GNB*

6) Who, then, can separate us from the love of Christ? Can trouble do it, or hardship or persecution or hunger or poverty or danger or death? ³⁶As the scripture says, "For your sake we are in danger of death at all times; we are treated like sheep that are going to be slaughtered." ³⁷**No, in all these things we have complete victory through him who loved us!** — *Romans 8:35-37 GNB*

7) You know how **I have worked with my own hands to make a living for myself** and my friends. — *Acts 20:34 CEV*

8) There is a real opportunity here for great and worthwhile **work,** even though there are many opponents. — *1 Corinthians 16:9 GNB*

111

9) We don't have the right to claim that we have done anything on our own. **God gives us what it takes to do all that we do.** — *2 Corinthians 3:5 CEV*

10) We often suffer, but we are never crushed. Even when we don't know what to do, we never give up. — *2 Corinthians 4:8 CEV*

11) We never give up. Our bodies are gradually dying, **but we ourselves are being made stronger each day.** — *2 Corinthians 4:16 CEV*

12) And this **small and temporary trouble we suffer** will bring us a **tremendous and eternal glory,** much greater than the trouble. — *2 Corinthians 4:17 GNB*

13) So let us not become tired of doing good; for if we do not give up, the time will come when we will **reap the harvest.** — *Galatians 6:9 GNB*

14) I ask God from the wealth of his glory **to give you power through his Spirit to be strong in your inner selves.** — *Ephesians 3:16 GNB*

15) If you are a thief, stop stealing. Be honest and work hard, so you will have something to give to people in need. — *Ephesians 4:28 CEV*

16) And I am convinced and sure of this very thing, **that He Who began a good work in you will continue until the day of Jesus Christ** [right up to the time of His return], **developing** [that good work] *and* **perfecting** *and* **bringing it to full completion in you.** — *Philippians 1:6 AMP*

17) His glorious power will make you patient and strong enough to endure anything, and you will be truly happy. [12] **I pray that you will be grateful to God** for letting you have part in what he has promised his people in the kingdom of light. — *Colossians 1:11-12 CEV*

18) **People who don't take care of their relatives, and especially their own families, have given up their faith.** They are **worse** than someone who doesn't have faith in the Lord. — *1 Timothy 5:8 CEV*

19) We do not want you to become lazy, **but to be like those who believe and are patient, and so receive what God has promised.** — *Hebrews 6:12 GNB*

20) **Keep on being brave!** It will bring you **great rewards.** — *Hebrews 10:35 CEV*

21) Consider it wholly joyful, my brethren, **whenever you are enveloped in or encounter trials of any sort or fall into various temptations.** ³Be assured and **understand that the trial and proving of your faith bring out endurance and steadfastness and patience.** ⁴But let endurance and steadfastness and patience have full play and **do a thorough work,** so that you may be [people] **perfectly and fully developed** [with no defects], lacking in nothing. — *James 1:2-4 AMP*

7e) Conquering The Challenges
You Face in Life

Read On: February 11th | April 28th | July 14th | September 29th | December 15th

1) If you completely obey these laws, the LORD your God will be loyal and keep the agreement he made with you, just as he promised our ancestors. — *Deuteronomy 7:12 CEV*

2) The Lord will love you and bless you by giving you many children and plenty of food, wine, and olive oil. Your herds of cattle **will have many calves,** and your flocks of sheep **will have many lambs.** — *Deuteronomy 7:13 CEV*

3) God will bless you more than any other nation — your families will **grow** and your livestock increase. — *Deuteronomy 7:14 CEV*

4) I know that **I will live to see the LORD'S goodness in this present life** — *Psalm 27:13 GNB*

5) Trust the LORD! Be brave and **strong** and trust the LORD. — *Psalm 27:14 CEV*

6) Hear my prayer, O God; don't turn away from my plea! — *Psalm 55:1 GNB*

7) Listen to me and answer me; I am worn out by my worries. — *Psalm 55:2 GNB*

8) As for me, I will call upon God, and the Lord will **save** me. — *Psalm 55:16 AMP*

9) He will bring me safely back from the battles that I **fight** against so many enemies. — *Psalm 55:18 GNB*

10) Leave your troubles with the LORD, and he will defend you; he never lets honest people be defeated. — *Psalm 55:22 GNB*

11) They that lie in wait for me would swallow me up or trample me all day long, **for they are many who fight against me, O Most High!** — *Psalm 56:2 AMP*

114

Scripture Therapy Daily Devotional For Men

12) When I am afraid, O LORD Almighty, I put my trust in you. ⁴I trust in God and am not afraid; I praise him for what he has promised. What can a mere human being do to me? — *Psalm 56:3-4 GNB*

13) My enemies make trouble for me all day long; they are always planning how to hurt me! — *Psalm 56:5 GNB*

14) You know how troubled I am; you have kept a record of my tears. Aren't they listed in your book? — *Psalm 56:8 GNB*

15) You protected me from death and kept me from stumbling, so that I would please you and follow the light that leads to life. — *Psalm 56:13 CEV*

16) But those who wait for the Lord [who expect, look for, and hope in Him] shall change and renew their strength and power; they shall lift their wings and mount up [close to God] as eagles [mount up to the sun]; they shall run and not be weary, they shall walk and not faint *or* become tired. — *Isaiah 40:31 AMP*

17) I have told you these things, so that in Me you may have [perfect] peace and confidence. In the world you have tribulation and trials and distress and frustration; but be of good cheer [take courage; be confident, certain, undaunted]! For I have overcome the world. [I have deprived it of power to harm you and have conquered it for you.] — *John 16:33 AMP*

18) What then shall we say to [all] this? If God is for us, who [can be] against us? [Who can be our foe, if God is on our side?] — *Romans 8:31 AMP*

19) Do all this in prayer, asking for God's help. Pray on every occasion, as the Spirit leads. For this reason keep alert and never give up; pray always for all God's people. — *Ephesians 6:18 GNB*

20) God cares for you, so turn all your worries over to him. — *1 Peter 5:7 CEV*

21) So whenever we are in need, we should come bravely before the throne of our merciful God. There we will be treated with undeserved kindness, and **we will find help.** — *Hebrews 4:16 CEV*

22) **Keep on being brave! It will bring you great rewards.** [36]Learn to be patient, so that you will please God and be given what he has **promised.**
— *Hebrews 10:35-36 CEV*

23) God cares for you, so **turn all your worries over to him.** — *1 Peter 5:7 CEV*

24) We are certain that God will hear our prayers when we ask for what pleases him. [15]And if we know that God listens when we pray, **we are sure that our prayers have already been answered.** — *1 John 5:14-15 CEV*

7f) Belief in God's Covenant
Promise to Bless You

Read On: February 12th | April 29th | July 15th | September 30th | December 16th

1) But you shall [earnestly] remember the Lord your God, for it is He Who gives you power to get wealth, **that He may establish His covenant** which He swore to your fathers, as it is this day.
— *Deuteronomy 8:18 AMP*

2) The LORD will give you a lot of children and make sure that your animals give birth to many young. The LORD promised your ancestors that this land would be yours, **and he will make it produce large crops for you.**
— *Deuteronomy 28:11 CEV*

3) The LORD will open the storehouses of the skies where he keeps the rain, and he will send rain on your land at just the right times. **He will make you successful in everything you do. You will have plenty of money to lend to other nations, but you won't need to borrow any yourself.** — *Deuteronomy 28:12 CEV*

4) But you must not reject any of his laws and teachings or worship other gods. — *Deuteronomy 28:14 CEV*

5) Israel, the LORD has made an agreement with you, **and if you keep your part, you will be successful in everything you do.**
— *Deuteronomy 29:9 CEV*

6) In this agreement, **the LORD promised that you would be his people and that he would be your God.** He first made this promise to your ancestors Abraham, Isaac, and Jacob, **and today the LORD is making this same promise to you.** But it isn't just for you; **it is also for your descendants.**
— *Deuteronomy 29:13-15 CEV*

7) Good people will prosper like palm trees, and they will grow strong like the cedars of Lebanon.
— *Psalm 92:12 CEV*

8) The Lord is always kind to those who worship him, and he keeps his promises to their descendants [18]**who faithfully obey him.** — *Psalm 103:17-18 CEV*

9) **Just be determined, be confident; and make sure that you obey the whole Law** that my servant Moses gave you. **Do not neglect any part of it and you will succeed wherever you go.** ⁸Be sure that the book of the Law is always read in your worship. **Study it day and night,** and make sure that you obey everything written in it. Then you will be prosperous and successful. — *Joshua 1:7-8 GNB*

10) **If you listen to me,** you will know what is right, just, and fair. **You will know what you should do.** — *Proverbs 2:9 GNB*

11) **I have taught you wisdom and the right way to live.** ¹²Nothing will stand in your way if you walk wisely, and **you will not stumble when you run.** — *Proverbs 4:11-12 GNB*

12) **Pay attention to what I say, my son. Listen to my words.** ²¹Never let them get away from you. Remember them and keep them in your heart. ²²**They will give life and health to anyone who understands them.** — *Proverbs 4:20-22 GNB*

13) **Ask the LORD to bless your plans,** and you will be **successful** in carrying them out. — *Proverbs 16:3 GNB*

14) Every mountain and hill may disappear. But **I will always be kind and merciful to you; I won't break my agreement to give your nation peace.** — *Isaiah 54:10 CEV*

15) The LORD says: "My people, I promise to give you my Spirit and my message. **These will be my gifts to you and your families forever. I, the LORD, have spoken."** — *Isaiah 59:21 CEV*

16) I am the LORD All-Powerful, **and I challenge you to put me to the test.** Bring the entire ten percent into the storehouse, so there will be food in my house. **Then I will open the windows of heaven and flood you with blessing after blessing.** — *Malachi 3:10 CEV*

17) I will also **stop locusts from destroying your crops** and keeping your vineyards from producing. ¹²Everyone of every nation will talk **about how I have blessed you** and about your wonderful land. **I, the LORD All-Powerful, have spoken!** — *Malachi 3:11-12 CEV*

18) And God is able to make all **grace (every favor and earthly blessing)** come to you in **abundance,** so that you may **always** and under all **circumstances** and whatever the need be self-sufficient [possessing enough to require no aid or support and furnished in abundance for every good work and charitable donation]. — *2 Corinthians 9:8 AMP*

19) You cannot fool God, so don't make a fool of yourself! **You will harvest what you plant.** ⁸If you follow your selfish desires, you will harvest destruction, but if you follow the Spirit, you will harvest eternal life. — *Galatians 6:7-8 CEV*

7g) Inspiration to Conquer
Your Fears and Doubts

Read On: February 13th | April 30th | July 16th | October 1st | December 17th

1) Live here, and I will be with you and bless you. I am going to give all this territory to you and to your descendants. I will keep the promise I made to your father Abraham. — *Genesis 26:3 GNB*

2) I will give you as many descendants as there are stars in the sky, and I will give them all this territory. All the nations will ask me to bless them as I have blessed your descendants. — *Genesis 26:4 GNB*

3) But Jabez prayed to the God of Israel, "Bless me, God, and give me much land. Be with me and keep me from anything evil that might cause me pain." And God gave him what he prayed for. — *1 Chronicles 4:10 GNB*

4) Ask the Lord to bless your plans, and you will be successful in carrying them out. — *Proverbs 16:3 GNB*

5) And I will always guide you and satisfy you with good things. I will keep you strong and well. You will be like a garden that has plenty of water, like a spring of water that never goes dry. — *Isaiah 58:11 GNB*

6) If you have faith when you pray, you will be given whatever you ask for." — *Matthew 21:22 CEV*

7) Everything you ask for in prayer will be yours, if you only have faith. — *Mark 11:24 CEV*

8) So I tell you to ask and you will receive, search and you will find, knock and the door will be opened for you. — *Luke 11:9 CEV*

9) Everyone who asks will receive, everyone who searches will find, and the door will be opened for everyone who knocks. — *Luke 11:10 CEV*

10) "Do not be afraid, little flock, for your Father is pleased to give you the Kingdom. — *Luke 12:32 GNB*

Scripture Therapy Daily Devotional For Men

11) John replied: **No one can do anything unless God in heaven allows it.** — *John 3:27 CEV*

12) **Ask me, and I will do whatever you ask.** This way the Son will bring honour to the Father. — *John 14:13 CEV*

13) **I will do whatever you ask me to do.** — *John 14:14 CEV*

14) You have not asked for anything in this way before, **but now you must ask in my name. Then it will be given to you, so that you will be completely happy.** — *John 16:24 CEV*

15) Since we are his children, **we will possess the blessings he keeps for his people,** and we will also **possess with Christ what God has kept for him;** for if we share Christ's suffering, we will also share his glory. — *Romans 8:17 GNB*

16) But it is just as the Scriptures say, **"What God has planned for people who love him is more than eyes have seen or ears have heard.** It has never even entered our minds!"— *1 Corinthians 2:9 CEV*

17) Who made you **superior** to others? **Didn't God give you everything you have?** Well, then, how can you boast, as if what you have **were not a gift?** — *1 Corinthians 4:7 GNB*

18) And God is able to make all **grace (every favor and earthly blessing) come to you in abundance,** so that you may **always** *and* under all **circumstances** *and* whatever the need be self-sufficient [possessing enough to require no aid or support and furnished in abundance for every good work and charitable donation]. — *2 Corinthians 9:8 AMP*

19) If you belong to Christ, then you are the descendants of Abraham and **will receive what God has promised.** — *Galatians 3:29 GNB*

20) **It was faith** that made Abraham able to become a father, even though he was too old and Sarah herself could not have children. **He trusted God to keep his promise.** — *Hebrews 11:11 GNB*

21) And I am convinced and sure of this very thing, **that He Who began a good work in you will continue until the day of Jesus Christ** [right up to the time of His return], developing [that good work] and **perfecting** and **bringing it to full completion in you.** — *Philippians 1:6 AMP*

22) I know what you do; I know that you have a little power; **you have followed my teaching and have been faithful to me. I have opened a door in front of you, which no one can close.** — *Revelation 3:8 GNB*

7h) Your Motivation to
Work Hard and Succeed

Read On: February 14th | May 1st | July 17th | October 2nd | December 18th

1) "If you obey the **LORD** your God and faithfully keep all his commands that I am giving you today, he will make you greater than any other nation on earth. — *Deuteronomy 28:1 GNB*

2) Instead, they find joy in **obeying the Law of the LORD, and they study it day and night.** — *Psalm 1:2 GNB*

3) Never let go of **loyalty** and **faithfulness.** Tie them round your neck; write them on your heart. ⁴If you do this, **both God and people will be pleased with you.** — *Proverbs 3:3-4 GNB*

4) How long is the lazy man going to lie in bed? When is he ever going to get up? ¹⁰"I'll just take a short nap," he says; "I'll fold my hands and rest a while." ¹¹But while he sleeps, poverty will attack him like an armed robber. — *Proverbs 6:9-11 GNB*

5) Being **lazy** will make you poor, **but hard work will make you rich.** — *Proverbs 10:4 GNB*

6) A hard-working farmer has **plenty to eat,** but it is stupid to **waste time on useless projects.** — *Proverbs 12:11 GNB*

7) Work hard, and you **will be a leader;** be lazy, and you will **end up** a slave. — *Proverbs 12:24 CEV*

8) Anyone too lazy to cook will starve, but a hard worker is a valuable treasure. — *Proverbs 12:27 CEV*

9) Ask the **LORD** to bless **your plans,** and you will be **successful** in carrying them out. — *Proverbs 16:3 GNB*

10) If you plan and work hard, you will have plenty; if you get in a hurry, you will end up poor. — *Proverbs 21:5 CEV*

11) Do you see a man **diligent** and **skillful in his business? He will stand before kings;** he will not stand before obscure men. — *Proverbs 22:29 AMP*

12) **Use wisdom and understanding to establish your home;** ⁴let good sense fill the rooms with priceless treasures. — *Proverbs 24:3-4 CEV*

13) Work hard, and you will have a lot of food; waste time, and you will have a lot of trouble. — *Proverbs 28:19 CEV*

14) God blesses his loyal people, but punishes all who want to get rich quick. — *Proverbs 28:20 CEV*

15) Cursed be he who does the work of the Lord negligently [with slackness, deceitfully]; and cursed be he who keeps back his sword from blood [in executing judgment pronounced by the Lord]. — *Jeremiah 48:10 AMP*

16) Therefore, my beloved brethren, **be firm (steadfast), immovable, always abounding in the work of the Lord** [always being superior, excelling, doing more than enough in the service of the Lord], knowing and being continually aware that your labor in the Lord is not futile [it is never wasted or to no purpose]. — *1 Corinthians 15:58 AMP*

17) Stay joined to me and let my teachings become part of you. Then you can pray for whatever you want, **and your prayer will be answered.** — *John 15:7 CEV*

18) Making the very most of the time [buying up each opportunity], because the days are evil. — *Ephesians 5:16 AMP*

19) Gladly serve your masters, as though they were the Lord himself, and not simply people. — *Ephesians 6:7 CEV*

20) At all times carry faith as a shield; for with it you will be able to **put out all the burning arrows shot by the Evil One.** — *Ephesians 6:16 GNB*

21) And so I am sure that God, who began this good work in you, will carry it on until it is finished on the Day of Christ Jesus.
— *Philippians 1:6 GNB*

22) My friends, I don't feel that I have already arrived. But I forget what is behind, and I struggle for what is ahead.
— *Philippians 3:13 CEV*

23) May you be made strong with all the strength which comes from his glorious power, so that you may be able to endure everything with patience. And with joy give thanks to the Father, who has made you fit to have your share of what God has reserved for his people in the kingdom of light. — *Colossians 1:11-12 GNB*

24) Do your best to win full approval in God's sight, as a worker who is not ashamed of his work, one who correctly teaches the message of God's truth.
— *2 Timothy 2:15 GNB*

25) And let our own [people really] learn to apply themselves to good deeds (to honest labor and honorable employment), so that they may be able to meet necessary demands whenever the occasion may require and not be living idle and uncultivated and unfruitful lives.
— *Titus 3:14 AMP*

26) But if any of you lack wisdom, you should pray to God, who will give it to you; because God gives generously and graciously to all.
— *James 1:5 GNB*

7i) Self-Belief to Succeed in
Everything You Do

Read On: February 15th | May 2nd | July 18th | October 3rd | December 19th

1) The LORD will make your businesses and your farms **successful**. — *Deuteronomy 28:3 CEV*

2) You will have many children. You will harvest large crops, and your herds of cattle and flocks of sheep and goats **will produce many young**. — *Deuteronomy 28:4 CEV*

3) The LORD will make you successful in your daily work. — *Deuteronomy 28:6 CEV*

4) The LORD will help you defeat your enemies and make them scatter in all directions. — *Deuteronomy 28:7 CEV*

5) The LORD your God is giving you the land, and he will make sure you are successful in everything you do. Your harvests will be so large that your storehouses will be full. — *Deuteronomy 28:8 CEV*

6) If you follow and obey the LORD, he will make you his own special people, just as he promised. — *Deuteronomy 28:9 CEV*

7) Be careful how you think; your life is shaped by your thoughts. — *Proverbs 4:23 GNB*

8) You, LORD, give **perfect peace** to those who **keep their purpose firm and put their trust in you.** — *Isaiah 26:3 GNB*

9) But those who trust in the LORD for help will find their strength renewed. They will rise on wings like eagles; they will run and not get weary; they will walk and not grow weak. — *Isaiah 40:31 GNB*

Scripture Therapy Daily Devotional For Men

10) Do not be afraid — I am with you! I am your God — let nothing terrify you! **I will make you strong and help you; I will protect you and save you.**
— *Isaiah 41:10 GNB*

11) You will seek me, and you will find me **because you will seek me with all your heart.**
— *Jeremiah 29:13 GNB*

12) He said to them, Because of the littleness of your faith [that is, your lack of firmly relying trust]. For truly I say to you, if you have faith [that is living] like a grain of mustard seed, you can say to this mountain, Move from here to yonder place, **and it will move; and nothing will be impossible to you.** — *Matthew 17:20 AMP*

13) Then Jesus said to his disciples, **"Why are you frightened? Have you still no faith?"**
— *Mark 4:40 GNB*

14) "Yes," said Jesus, "if you yourself can! **Everything is possible for the person who has faith."** — *Mark 9:23 GNB*

15) And **Jesus,** replying, said to them, **Have faith in God [constantly].** — *Mark 11:22 AMP*

16) Jesus said to her, Did I not tell you and promise you **that if you would believe** and **rely on Me,** you would **see the glory of God?**
— *John 11:40 AMP*

17) His faith did not leave him, and he did not doubt God's promise; his faith filled him with power, and he gave praise to God. ²¹**He was absolutely sure that God would be able to do what he had promised.** ²²That is why Abraham, through faith, "was accepted as righteous by God." — *Romans 4:20–22 GNB*

18) And **God,** who supplies seed to sow and bread to eat, **will also supply you with all the seed you need** and **will make it grow** and produce a rich **harvest** from your generosity. — *2 Corinthians 9:10 GNB*

19) Do not fret or have any **anxiety about anything,** but in every circumstance and in everything, by prayer and petition (definite requests), **with thanksgiving, continue to make your wants known to God.** — *Philippians 4:6 AMP*

20) I have strength for all things in Christ Who empowers me **[I am ready for anything and equal to anything through Him Who infuses inner strength into me; I am self— sufficient in Christ's sufficiency].** — *Philippians 4:13 AMP*

21) Dear friends, you must never become tired of doing right. — *2 Thessalonians 3:13 CEV*

22) No one can please God **without faith,** for whoever comes to God must have faith that God exists and rewards those who seek him. — *Hebrews 11:6 GNB*

23) Be alert, be on the watch! Your enemy, the Devil, roams round like a roaring lion, **looking for someone to devour.** ⁹**Be firm in your faith and resist him,** because you know that your fellow— believers in all the world are going through the same kind of sufferings. — *1 Peter 5:8–9 GNB*

24) For our love for God means that we obey his commands. And his commands are not too hard for us, — *1 John 5:3 GNB*

7j) Confidence in God to Provide for Your Needs

Read On: February 16th | May 3rd | July 19th | October 4th | December 20th

1) Live here, and I will be with you and bless you. I am going to give all this territory to you and to your descendants. I will keep the promise I made to your father Abraham. — *Genesis 26:3 GNB*

2) You know that the LORD your God is the only true God. So love him and obey his commands, and he will faithfully keep his agreement with you and your descendants for a thousand generations. — *Deuteronomy 7:9 CEV*

3) When you become successful, don't say, "I'm rich, and I've earned it all myself." — *Deuteronomy 8:17 CEV*

4) Love the LORD your God, obey him and be faithful to him, and then you and your descendants will live long in the land that he promised to give your ancestors, Abraham, Isaac, and Jacob." — *Deuteronomy 30:20 GNB*

5) Always let him lead you, and he will clear the road for you to follow. — *Proverbs 3:6 CEV*

6) Being lazy will make you poor, but hard work will make you rich. — *Proverbs 10:4 GNB*

7) Be generous, and you will be prosperous. Help others, and you will be helped. — *Proverbs 11:25 GNB*

8) Work hard, and you will be a leader; be lazy, and you will end up a slave. — *Proverbs 12:24 CEV*

9) Suppose you are very rich and able to enjoy everything you own. Then go ahead and enjoy working hard — this is God's gift to you. — *Ecclesiastes 5:19 CEV*

10) If you willingly obey me, the best crops in the land will be yours. — *Isaiah 1:19 CEV*

11) You, LORD, give perfect peace to those who keep their purpose firm and put their trust in you. — *Isaiah 26:3 GNB*

12) I, the LORD, love justice! But I hate robbery and injustice. **My people, I solemnly promise to reward you with an eternal agreement.** — *Isaiah 61:8 CEV*

13) Your descendants will be known in every nation. **All who see them will realize that they have been blessed, by me, the Lord.** — *Isaiah 61:9 CEV*

14) And whenever you stand praying, **if you have anything against anyone, forgive him and let it drop (leave it, let it go), in order that your Father Who is in heaven may also forgive you your [own] failings and shortcomings and let them drop.** ²⁶*But if you do not forgive, neither will your Father in heaven forgive your failings and shortcomings.* — *Mark 11:25-26 AMP*

15) **Give to others,** and God will give to you. **Indeed, you will receive a full measure, a generous helping, poured into your hands — all that you can hold.** The measure you use for others is the one that God will use for you." — *Luke 6:38 GNB*

16) Each of you must make up your own mind about how much to give. But don't feel sorry that you must give and **don't feel that you are forced to give. God loves people who love to give.** — *2 Corinthians 9:7 CEV*

17) And God is able to give you more than you need, so that you will always have **all you need for yourselves** and more than enough for every good cause. — *2 Corinthians 9:8 GNB*

18) And become **useful** and **helpful** and **kind to one another, tenderhearted (compassionate, understanding, loving-hearted), forgiving one another** [readily and freely], as God in Christ forgave you. — *Ephesians 4:32 AMP*

19) Don't worry about anything, but in all your prayers **ask God for what you need,** always asking him with a thankful heart. — *Philippians 4:6 GNB*

21) **Be tolerant with one another** and **forgive** one another whenever any of you has a complaint against someone else. **You must forgive one another just as the Lord has forgiven you.** — *Colossians 3:13 GNB*

20) In conclusion, my brothers and sisters, **fill your minds with those things that are good and that deserve praise:** things that are **true, noble, right, pure, lovely,** and **honourable.** — *Philippians 4:8 GNB*

22) Let your character or moral disposition be free from love of money [including greed, avarice, lust, and craving for earthly possessions] and be satisfied with your present [circumstances and with what you have]; for He [God] Himself has said, **I will not in any way fail you nor give you up nor leave you without support.** [I will] not, [I will] not, [I will] not in any degree leave you helpless nor forsake nor let [you] down (relax My hold on you)! [Assuredly not!] — *Hebrews 13:5 AMP*

23) **I pray that God will be kind to you and will let you live in perfect peace!** May you keep learning more and more **about God and our Lord Jesus.** — *2 Peter 1:2 CEV*

7k) Your Confidence and Determination to Succeed

Read On: February 17th | May 4th | July 20th | October 5th | December 21st

1) I am now giving you **the choice** between life and death, between **God's blessing** and God's curse, and I call heaven and earth to witness the choice you make. **Choose life.** — *Deuteronomy 30:19 GNB*

2) No man shall be able to **stand before you** all the days of your life. **As I was with Moses, so I will be with you; I will not fail you or forsake you.** — *Joshua 1:5 AMP*

3) Just be determined, be confident; and make sure that you obey the whole Law that my servant Moses gave you. Do not neglect any part of it and you will succeed wherever you go. — *Joshua 1:7 GNB*

4) **This Book of the Law shall not depart out of your mouth, but you shall meditate on it day and night,** that you may **observe** and **do according to all that is written in it.** For then you shall make your way prosperous, and then **you shall deal wisely and have good success.** — *Joshua 1:8 AMP*

5) Remember that **I have commanded you to be determined and confident!** Don't be afraid or discouraged, **for I, the LORD your God, am with you wherever you go."** — *Joshua 1:9 GNB*

6) **The LORD helped David,** and he and his soldiers always won their battles. — *1 Samuel 18:14 CEV*

7) Now, Job, **make peace with God** and **stop treating him like an enemy;** if you do, then he will **bless you.** — *Job 22:21 GNB*

8) **Always let him lead you,** and he will **clear the road for you to follow.** — *Proverbs 3:6 CEV*

9) When the LORD blesses you with riches, you have **nothing to regret.** — *Proverbs 10:22 CEV*

10) **God is my saviour; I will trust him and not be afraid.** The LORD gives me power and strength; he is my saviour. — *Isaiah 12:2 GNB*

11) And Jesus, replying, said to them, **Have faith in God [constantly].** — *Mark 11:22 AMP*

12) **If you confess that Jesus is Lord** and believe that **God raised him from death, you will be saved.** — *Romans 10:9 GNB*

13) As the scripture says, **"Everyone who calls out to the Lord for help will be saved."** — *Romans 10:13 GNB*

14) God can bless you with everything you need, and you will always have more than enough to do all kinds of **good things** for others. — *2 Corinthians 9:8 CEV*

15) **You were saved by faith in God,** who treats us much better than we deserve. **This is God's gift to you,** and not anything you have done on your own. ⁹It isn't something you have **earned,** so there is nothing you can boast about. — *Ephesians 2:8-9 CEV*

16) **God has made us what we are,** and in our union with **Christ Jesus he has created us for a life of good deeds, which he has already prepared for us to do.** — *Ephesians 2:10 GNB*

17) **His glorious power will make you patient and strong enough to endure anything, and you will be truly happy.** ¹²I pray that you will be grateful to God for letting you have part in what he has promised his people in the kingdom of light. — *Colossians 1:11-12 CEV*

18) **I have fought well. I have finished the race,** and **I have been faithful.** — *2 Timothy 4:7 CEV*

19) But without faith no one can please God. We must believe that **God is real** and that **he rewards** everyone who searches for him. — *Hebrews 11:6 CEV*

20) Let the wonderful kindness and the understanding that come from our Lord and Saviour Jesus Christ help you to keep on growing. Praise Jesus now and forever! Amen. — *2 Peter 3:18 CEV*

21) **But if we confess our sins to God,** he will keep his promise and do what is right: **he will forgive us our sins and purify us from all our wrongdoing.**
— *1 John 1:9 GNB*

CHAPTER 8

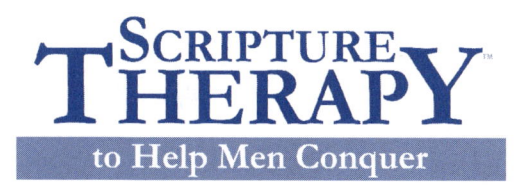

Scripture Therapy™ to Help Men Conquer Personality Issues

TOPICS

8a) Patience in Listening to Other People's Views
Read On: February 18th | May 5th | July 21st | October 6th | December 22nd

8b) Having a Gentle Personality
Read On: February 19th | May 6th | July 22nd | October 7th | December 23rd

8c) Removing Bad Habits From Your Personality
Read On: February 20th | May 7th | July 23rd | October 8th | December 24th

8d) Developing a Christian Personality
Read On: February 21st | May 8th | July 24th | October 9th | December 25th

8e) Having a Confident Personality
Read On: February 22nd | May 9th | July 25th | October 10th | December 26th

8f) Having a Personality That Pleases The Lord
Read On: February 23rd | May 10th | July 26th | October 11th | December 27th

8a) Patience in Listening to
Other People's Views

Read On: February 18th | May 5th | July 21st | October 6th | December 22nd

1) My child, **obey the teachings of your parents.** — *Proverbs 1:8 CEV*

2) If you do this, **both God and people will be pleased with you.** — *Proverbs 3:4 GNB*

3) **Never let yourself think that you are wiser than you are;** simply obey the LORD and refuse to do wrong. — *Proverbs 3:7 GNB*

4) My child, **if you listen and obey my teachings, you will live a long time.** — *Proverbs 4:10 CEV*

5) There are six or seven kinds of people the LORD doesn't like: ¹⁷Those who are **too proud or tell lies or murder,** ¹⁸those who **make evil plans** or **are quick to do wrong,** ¹⁹those who tell lies in court or stir up trouble in a family. — *Proverbs 6:16-19 CEV*

6) **Obey the teaching of your parents** – ²¹always **keep it in mind** and never **forget it**. ²²Their teaching will **guide you** when you walk, **protect you** when you sleep, and **talk to you** when you are awake. — *Proverbs 6:20-22 CEV*

7) The Law of the Lord is a lamp, and its teachings shine brightly. **Correction and self-control will lead you through life.** — *Proverbs 6:23 CEV*

8) If you have good **sense, you will listen and obey;** if all you do is talk, you will destroy yourself. — *Proverbs 10:8 CEV*

9) **Accept correction, and you will find life;** reject correction, and **you will miss the road.** — *Proverbs 10:17 CEV*

10) **People who are proud will soon be disgraced.** It is wiser to be modest. — *Proverbs 11:2 GNB*

11) **Fools** think they know what is best, **but a sensible person listens to advice.** — *Proverbs 12:15 CEV*

12) Evil people are proud and arrogant, but sin is the only crop they produce.
— *Proverbs 21:4 CEV*

13) Listening to good advice is worth much more than jewellery made of gold. — *Proverbs 25:12 CEV*

14) It makes good sense to obey the Law of God, but you disgrace your parents if you make friends with worthless nobodies.
— *Proverbs 28:7 CEV*

15) Only fools would trust what they alone think, but if you live by wisdom, you will do all right. — *Proverbs 28:26 CEV*

16) If you keep being stubborn after many warnings, you will suddenly discover you have gone too far. — *Proverbs 29:1 CEV*

17) Our holy God lives forever in the highest heavens, and this is what he says: Though I live high above in the holy place, I am here to help those who are humble and depend only on me.
— *Isaiah 57:15 CEV*

18) Whoever is the greatest should be the servant of the others. — *Matthew 23:11 CEV*

19) Whoever exalts himself [with haughtiness and empty pride] shall be humbled (brought low), and whoever humbles himself [whoever has a modest opinion of himself and behaves accordingly] shall be raised to honor.
— *Matthew 23:12 AMP*

20) And because of God's gracious gift to me I say to every one of you: Do not think of yourself more highly than you should. Instead, be modest in your thinking, and judge yourself according to the amount of faith that God has given you. — *Romans 12:3 GNB*

21) Do your own work well, and then you will have something to be proud of. But don't compare yourself with others. — *Galatians 6:4 CEV*

22) God loves you and has chosen you as his own special people. **So be gentle, kind, humble, meek, and patient.**

— *Colossians 3:12 CEV*

23) Put up with each other, and **forgive anyone who does you wrong,** just as Christ has **forgiven** you. — *Colossians 3:13 CEV*

24) Be humble when you correct people who oppose you. Perhaps God will lead them to turn to him and learn the truth. — *2 Timothy 2:25 CEV*

8b) Having
A Gentle Personality

Read On: February 19th | May 6th | July 22nd | October 7th | December 23rd

1) Giving the **right answer** at the **right time** makes everyone **happy.** — *Proverbs 15:23 CEV*

2) **Kind words** are like honey — **they cheer you up** and make you feel **strong.** — *Proverbs 16:24 CEV*

3) It is better to be **patient** than **powerful.** It is better to **win control over yourself** than over whole cities. — *Proverbs 16:32 GNB*

4) But I tell you to **love your enemies** and **pray** for **anyone** who **ill-treats** you. — *Matthew 5:44 CEV*

5) "**If you forgive others the wrongs they have done to you,** your Father in heaven **will also forgive you.** ¹⁵But if you do not forgive others, then your Father will not forgive the wrongs you have done. — *Matthew 6:14-15 GNB*

6) bless those who curse you, and pray for those who ill-treat you. — *Luke 6:28 GNB*

7) Give to others, and God will give to you. Indeed, you will receive a full measure, a generous helping, poured into your hands — all that you can hold. The measure you use for others is the one that God will use for you." — *Luke 6:38 GNB*

8) If you forgive people's **sins,** they are forgiven; if you do not forgive them, they are not forgiven." — *John 20:23 GNB*

9) If someone has done you **wrong,** do not repay him with a wrong. Try to do what everyone considers to be good. — *Romans 12:17 GNB*

10) Do your best to preserve the unity which the Spirit **gives** by means of the **peace** that binds you together. — *Ephesians 4:3 GNB*

11) And become **useful** and **helpful** and **kind to one another,** tenderhearted (compassionate, understanding, loving-hearted), forgiving one another [readily and freely], as God in Christ forgave you. — *Ephesians 4:32 AMP*

12) Your life must be controlled by love, just as Christ loved us and gave his life for us as a sweet-smelling offering and sacrifice that pleases God. — *Ephesians 5:2 GNB*

13) Act like people with good sense and not like fools. — *Ephesians 5:15 CEV*

14) Always be gentle with others. The Lord will soon be here. — *Philippians 4:5 CEV*

15) Finally, my friends, keep your minds on whatever is true, pure, right, holy, friendly, and proper. Don't ever stop thinking about what is truly worthwhile and worthy of praise. — *Philippians 4:8 CEV*

16) and God's servants must not be troublemakers. They must be kind to everyone, and they must be good teachers and very patient. — *2 Timothy 2:24 CEV*

17) Try to be at peace with everyone, and try to live a holy life, because no one will see the Lord without it. — *Hebrews 12:14 GNB*

18) Obey your leaders and do what they say. They are watching over you, and they must answer to God. So don't make them sad as they do their work. Make them happy. Otherwise, they won't be able to help you at all. — *Hebrews 13:17 CEV*

19) In fact, God treats us with even greater kindness, just as the Scriptures say, "God opposes everyone who is proud, but he is kind to everyone who is humble." — *James 4:6 CEV*

20) Don't be bossy to those people who are in your care, but set an example for them. — *1 Peter 5:3 CEV*

21) All of you young people should obey your elders. In fact, everyone should be humble towards everyone else. The Scriptures say, "God opposes proud people, **but he helps everyone who is humble.**" — *1 Peter 5:5 CEV*

22) Therefore humble yourselves **[demote, lower yourselves in your own estimation]** under the mighty hand of God, that in due time **He may exalt you,** — *1 Peter 5:6 AMP*

23) No man has at any time [yet] seen God. **But if we love one another,** God abides **(lives and remains) in us** and His love (that love which is essentially His) is brought to completion **(to its full maturity,** runs its full course, **is perfected) in us!** — *1 John 4:12 AMP*

8c) Removing Bad Habits From Your Personality

Read On: February 20th | May 7th | July 23rd | October 8th | December 24th

1) **Envy** and **jealousy** will kill a **stupid fool.** — *Job 5:2 CEV*

2) How long is the lazy man going to lie in bed? When is he ever going to get up? 10"I'll just take a short nap," he says; "I'll fold my hands and rest a while." 11But while he sleeps, **poverty will attack him** like an armed robber. — *Proverbs 6:9-11 GNB*

3) Being **lazy** will make you **poor,** but **hard work** will make you **rich.** — *Proverbs 10:4 GNB*

4) If you stay calm, you are **wise,** but if you have a **hot temper,** you only show how **stupid** you are. — *Proverbs 14:29 GNB*

5) Hot tempers cause **arguments,** but **patience** brings **peace.** — *Proverbs 15:18 GNB*

6) Too much pride causes trouble. **Be sensible and take advice.** — *Proverbs 13:10 CEV*

7) If you reject God's teaching, you will pay the price; if you **obey his commands,** you will be **rewarded.** — *Proverbs 13:13 CEV*

8) All who refuse correction will be poor and disgraced; all who **accept correction** will be **praised.** — *Proverbs 13:18 CEV*

9) **Honest correction** is appreciated more than flattery. — *Proverbs 28:23 CEV*

10) Correct your children, and they will be wise; children **out of control** disgrace their mothers. — *Proverbs 29:15 CEV*

11) I promise you that on the day of judgment, **everyone will have to account for every careless word they have spoken.** — *Matthew 12:36 CEV*

12) Do not conform yourselves to the standards of this world, but let God **transform you inwardly** by a **complete change of your mind.** Then you will be **able to know the will of God** — what is **good** and is **pleasing to him** and is **perfect.** — *Romans 12:2 GNB*

13) My friends, God has made us these promises. **So we should stay away from everything that keeps our bodies and spirits from being clean.** We should **honour God** and **try to be completely like him.** — *2 Corinthians 7:1 CEV*

14) As for you, my brothers and sisters, you were called to be free. But do not let this freedom become an excuse for letting your physical desires control you. Instead, **let love make you serve one another.** — *Galatians 5:13 GNB*

15) You were told that your **foolish desires** will **destroy you** and that **you must give up your old way of life** with all its **bad habits.** — *Ephesians 4:22 CEV*

16) Let the Spirit change your way of thinking ²⁴and make you into a new person. You were created to be like God, and so you must **please him and be truly holy.** — *Ephesians 4:23-24 CEV*

17) Stop being bitter and an**gry** with others. Don't **yell** at one another or **curse** each other or ever be **rude.** — *Ephesians 4:31 CEV*

18) You yourselves used to be in the darkness, but since you have become the **Lord's** people, you are in the light. **So you must live like people who belong to the light.** — *Ephesians 5:8 GNB*

19) Don't destroy yourself by getting drunk, but let the Spirit fill your life. — *Ephesians 5:18 CEV*

20) **He taught us to give up our wicked ways and our worldly desires** and to live **decent and honest lives** in this world. — *Titus 2:12 CEV*

21) My brothers and sisters, as believers in our Lord Jesus Christ, the Lord of glory, **you must never treat people in different ways according to their outward appearance.** — *James 2:1 GNB*

22) For you know **what was paid to set you free from the worthless manner of life handed down by your ancestors.** It was not something that can be destroyed, such as silver or gold. — *1 Peter 1:18 GNB*

8d) Developing
A Christian Personality

Read On: February 21st | May 8th | July 24th | October 9th | December 25th

1) How can young people keep their lives pure? By obeying your commands. — *Psalm 119:9 GNB*

2) Be careful **how you think;** your life is shaped **by your thoughts.** — *Proverbs 4:23 GNB*

3) Try hard to do right, and you will win friends; go looking for trouble, and you will find it. — *Proverbs 11:27 CEV*

4) Show me someone **who does a good job,** and I will show you someone **who is better than most and worthy of the company of kings.** — *Proverbs 22:29 GNB*

5) Without wood, a fire goes out; **without gossip, quarreling stops.** — *Proverbs 26:20 GNB*

6) Better is the end of a thing than the beginning of it, and **the patient in spirit is better than the proud in spirit.** — *Ecclesiastes 7:8 AMP*

7) And the seeds sown in the good soil stand for **those who hear the message and understand it: they bear fruit,** some as much as one hundred, others sixty, and others thirty." — *Matthew 13:23 GNB*

8) Keep watch and **pray that you will not fall into temptation.** The spirit is willing, **but the flesh is weak.**" — *Matthew 26:41 GNB*

9) And when you stand and pray, forgive anything you may have against anyone, so that your Father in heaven will forgive the wrongs you have done." — *Mark 11:25 GNB*

10) For they loved the approval and the **praise** and **the glory that come from men** [instead of and] more than **the glory that comes from God.** [They valued their credit with men more than their credit with God.] — *John 12:43 AMP*

11) And so, each of us must give an account to God for what we do. — *Romans 14:12 CEV*

12) **Love endures long** and is patient and kind; love never is **envious** nor boils over with **jealousy,** is not **boastful** or vainglorious, **does not display itself haughtily.** ⁵It is not conceited **(arrogant and inflated with pride)**; it is not **rude** (unmannerly) and **does not act unbecomingly.** Love (God's love in us) **does not insist on its own rights** or **its own way,** for it is not **self- seeking;** it is not **touchy** or fretful or **resentful;** it **takes no account of the evil done to it** [it **pays no attention** to a suffered wrong]. — *1 Corinthians 13:4- 5 AMP*

13) It is **love,** then, that you **should strive for. Set your hearts on spiritual gifts,** especially the gift of proclaiming God's message. — *1 Corinthians 14:1 GNB*

14) We are not trying to dictate to you what you must believe; **we know that you stand firm in the faith.** Instead, **we are working with you for your own happiness.** — *2 Corinthians 1:24 GNB*

15) God is working in you to make you **willing and able to obey him.** — *Philippians 2:13 CEV*

16) God's Spirit makes us loving, happy, peaceful, patient, kind, good, faithful, ²³**gentle, and self- controlled.** There is no law against behaving in any of these ways. ²⁴**And because we belong to Christ Jesus, we have killed our selfish feelings and desires.** ²⁵God's Spirit has given us life, and so we should follow the Spirit. — *Galatians 5:22-25 CEV*

17) Keep away from profane and foolish discussions, which only drive people further away from God. — *2 Timothy 2:16 GNB*

18) Make sure that no one **misses out on God's wonderful kindness.** Don't let anyone become bitter and cause **trouble for the rest of you.** — *Hebrews 12:15 CEV*

19) After all, God chose you to suffer as you follow in the footsteps of Christ, who set an example by suffering for you. — *1 Peter 2:21 CEV*

20) Although he was abused, he never tried to get even. And when he suffered, **he made no threats.** Instead, **he had faith in God,** who judges fairly. — *1 Peter 2:23 CEV*

21) Just as shepherds watch over their sheep, **you must watch over everyone God has placed in your care.** Do it willingly in order to please God, and not simply because you think you must. **Let it be something you want to do,** instead of something you do **merely to make money.** — *1 Peter 5:2 CEV*

8e) Having
A Confident Personality

Read On: February 22nd | May 9th | July 25th | October 10th | December 26th

1) Be sure that the book of the Law is always read in your worship. Study it day and night, and make sure that you obey everything written in it. Then you will be **prosperous** and **successful**. — *Joshua 1:8 GNB*

2) Remember that I have commanded you to be determined and confident! Don't be afraid or discouraged, for I, the LORD your God, am with you wherever you go." — *Joshua 1:9 GNB*

3) Wait and **hope for** and **expect** the Lord; be **brave** and **of good courage** and let your heart be **stout** and **enduring**. Yes, **wait for** and **hope for** and **expect** the Lord. — *Psalm 27:14 AMP*

4) Do what the Lord wants, and he will give you your heart's desire. — *Psalm 37:4 CEV*

5) Be **careful** how you **think**; your **life** is **shaped** by your **thoughts**. — *Proverbs 4:23 GNB*

6) When people are happy, they smile, but when they are **sad**, they look depressed. — *Proverbs 15:13 GNB*

7) Everyone with good sense **wants to learn.** — *Proverbs 18:15 CEV*

8) Obey the Lord's teachings and you will live — disobey and you will die. — *Proverbs 19:16 CEV*

9) If you **stop learning,** you will forget what you already know. — *Proverbs 19:27 CEV*

10) Be sure you have sound advice before making plans or starting a war. — *Proverbs 20:18 CEV*

11) If you **plan** and **work hard, you will** have plenty; if you get in a **hurry,** you will end up poor. — *Proverbs 21:5 CEV*

12) Battles are won by listening to advice and making a lot of plans. — *Proverbs 24:6 CEV*

13) The wicked run when no one is chasing them, but **an honest person** is as **brave** as a **lion.**
— *Proverbs 28:1 GNB*

14) But those who wait for the Lord **[who expect, look for, and hope in Him]** shall **change** and **renew** their **strength** and **power;** they shall lift their wings and mount up [close to God] as eagles [mount up to the sun]; **they shall run and not be weary, they shall walk and not faint or become tired.** — *Isaiah 40:31 AMP*

15) For this reason we never become discouraged. Even though our physical being is gradually decaying, yet our **spiritual being is renewed day after day.** — *2 Corinthians 4:16 GNB*

16) For this reason I am telling you, whatever you ask for in prayer, **believe (trust and be confident) that it is granted to you,** and **you will [get it].**
— *Mark 11:24 AMP*

17) Do not fret or have any anxiety about anything, but in every circumstance and in everything, **by prayer and petition** (definite requests), with thanksgiving, **continue to make your wants known to God.** — *Philippians 4:6 AMP*

18) So we take comfort and are encouraged and **confidently** and **boldly say, The Lord is my Helper;** I will not be seized with alarm **[I will not fear or dread or be terrified]. What can man do to me?**
— *Hebrews 13:6 AMP*

19) My brothers and sisters, consider yourselves fortunate when all kinds of trials come your way, ³**for you know that when your faith succeeds in facing such trials, the result is the ability to endure.**
— *James 1:2–3 GNB*

8f) Having a Personality That Pleases **The Lord**

Read On: February 23rd | May 10th | July 26th | October 11th | December 27th

1) She kept begging Joseph day after day, **but he refused to do what she wanted or even to go near her.** — *Genesis 39:10 CEV*

2) I am now giving you the choice between life and death, **between God's blessing and God's curse, and I call heaven and earth to witness the choice you make. Choose life.** — *Deuteronomy 30:19 GNB*

3) Give me again the joy that comes from your salvation, and make me willing to obey you. ¹³Then I will **teach** sinners your commands, and they will turn back to you. — *Psalm 51:12-13 GNB*

4) I worship you with all my heart. Don't let me walk away from your commands. — *Psalm 119:10 CEV*

5) I treasure your word above all else; it keeps me **from sinning against you.** — *Psalm 119:11 CEV*

6) I want to obey your commands; give me new life, for you are righteous. — *Psalm 119:40 GNB*

7) With wisdom you will learn what is right and honest and fair. — *Proverbs 2:9 CEV*

8) Carefully guard your thoughts because they are the **source of true life.** — *Proverbs 4:23 CEV*

9) They get lost and die **because of their foolishness and lack of self-control.** — *Proverbs 5:23 CEV*

10) If you turn from the right way, you will be punished; if you refuse correction, you will die. — *Proverbs 15:10 CEV*

11) so that it is no longer I who live, **but it is Christ who lives in me.** This life that I live now, **I live by faith in the Son of God, who loved me and gave his life for me.** — *Galatians 2:20 GNB*

Scripture Therapy Daily Devotional For Men

12) He did this **to prepare all God's people for the work of Christian service, in order to build up the body of Christ.** — *Ephesians 4:12 GNB*

13) Instead, by speaking the truth in a spirit of love, we must **grow up in every way to Christ, who is the head.** — *Ephesians 4:15 GNB*

14) Since you are God's dear children, **you must try to be like him.** — *Ephesians 5:1 GNB*

15) Children, it is your **Christian duty** to **obey your parents,** for this is the **right thing to do.** — *Ephesians 6:1 GNB*

16) Your lives will be filled with the **truly good qualities** which **only Jesus Christ can produce,** for the glory and praise of God. — *Philippians 1:11 GNB*

17) Now make me completely happy! **Live in harmony by showing love for each other. Be united in what you think,** as if you were only one person. — *Philippians 2:2 CEV*

18) My dear friends, you always obeyed when I was with you. Now that I am away, you should obey even more. **So work with fear and trembling to discover what it really means to be saved.** — *Philippians 2:12 CEV*

19) The **attitude** you should have **is the one that Christ Jesus had:** — *Philippians 2:5 GNB*

20) because **God is always at work in you** to make you **willing** and able **to obey his own purpose.** — *Philippians 2:13 GNB*

21) Always be gentle with others. The Lord will soon be here. — *Philippians 4:5 CEV*

22) Your speech should always be pleasant and interesting, and you should know how to give **the right answer** to everyone. — *Colossians 4:6 GNB*

23) That you may walk **(live and conduct yourselves) in a manner worthy of the Lord, fully pleasing to Him** and desiring to please Him in all things, bearing fruit in **every good work** and steadily growing *and* increasing in *and* by the knowledge of God [with fuller, deeper, and clearer insight, acquaintance, and recognition]. — *Colossians 1:10 AMP*

24) **Do your best to win full approval in God's sight,** as a worker **who is not ashamed of his work,** one who correctly teaches the message of God's truth.
— *2 Timothy 2:15 GNB*

25) Not many [of you] **should become teachers** (self-constituted censors and reprovers of others), my brethren, for you know that **we [teachers] will be judged by a higher standard** and with **greater severity** [than other people; thus we assume the **greater accountability** and the more condemnation]. — *James 3:1 AMP*

CHAPTER 9

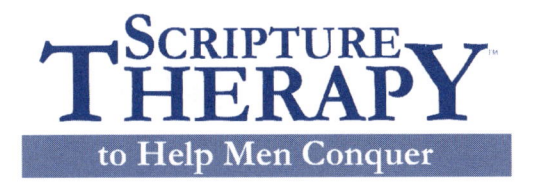

Scripture Therapy™ to Help Men Conquer
LIFESTYLE ISSUES

TOPICS

9a) Living a Christian Lifestyle
Read On: February 24th | May 11th | July 27th | October 12th | December 28th

9b) Living a Lifestyle That Pleases The Lord
Read On: February 25th | May 12th | July 28th | October 13th | December 29th

9c) Help Conquering Your Bad Habits
Read On: February 26th | May 13th | July 29th | October 14th | December 30th

9d) Learning to Live a Pure and Holy Lifestyle
Read On: February 27th | May 14th | July 30th | October 15th | December 31st

9e) Making Positive Changes to Your Lifestyle
Read On: February 28th | May 15th | July 31st | October 16th |

9a) Living a
Christian Lifestyle

Read On: February 24th | May 11th | July 27th | October 12th | December 28th

1) Create a pure heart in me, O God, and put a new and loyal spirit in me. — *Psalm 51:10 GNB*

2) Carefully guard your thoughts because they are the source of true life. — *Proverbs 4:23 CEV*

3) Whoever exalts himself [with haughtiness and empty pride] shall be humbled (brought low), and whoever humbles himself [whoever has a modest opinion of himself and behaves accordingly] shall be raised to honor. — *Matthew 23:12 AMP*

4) But you do not live as your human nature tells you to; instead, you live as the Spirit tells you to — if, in fact, God's Spirit lives in you. Whoever does not have the Spirit of Christ does not belong to him. — *Romans 8:9 GNB*

5) But take up the weapons of the Lord Jesus Christ, and stop paying attention to your sinful nature and satisfying its desires. — *Romans 13:14 GNB*

6) Someone will say, "I am allowed to do anything." Yes; but not everything is good for you. I could say that I am allowed to do anything, but I am not going to let anything make me its slave. — *1 Corinthians 6:12 GNB*

7) For no temptation (no trial regarded as enticing to sin), [no matter how it comes or where it leads] has overtaken you and laid hold on you that is not common to man [that is, no temptation or trial has come to you that is beyond human resistance and that is not adjusted and adapted and belonging to human experience, and such as man can bear]. But God is faithful [to His Word and to His compassionate nature], and He [can be trusted] not to let you be tempted and tried and assayed beyond your ability and strength of resistance and power to endure, but with the temptation He will [always] also provide the way out (the means of escape to a landing place), that you may be capable and strong and powerful to bear up under it patiently. — *1 Corinthians 10:13 AMP*

Scripture Therapy Daily Devotional For Men

8) Therefore put on God's complete armor, **that you may be able to resist and stand your ground on the evil day [of danger],** and, having done all [the crisis demands], **to stand [firmly in your place].** — *Ephesians 6:13 AMP*

9) In conclusion, my brothers and sisters, **fill your minds with those things that are good** and that deserve praise: **things that are true, noble, right, pure, lovely, and honourable.** — *Philippians 4:8 GNB*

10) Learn to be patient, so that you will please God and be given what he has promised. — *Hebrews 10:36 CEV*

11) Obey your leaders and do what they say. They are watching over you, and they must answer to God. So don't make them sad as they do their work. **Make them happy.** Otherwise, they won't be able to help you at all. — *Hebrews 13:17 CEV*

12) All of us do many wrong things. **But if you can control your tongue,** you are **mature** and **able to control your whole body.** — *James 3:2 CEV*

13) So then, **submit to God. Resist the Devil,** and he will run away from you. — *James 4:7 GNB*

14) Come near to God, and he will come near to you. Wash your hands, you sinners! **Purify your hearts,** you hypocrites! — *James 4:8 GNB*

15) Be patient, then, my brothers and sisters, until the Lord comes. See how patient a farmer is **as he waits for his land to produce precious crops.** He waits **patiently** for the autumn and spring rains. — *James 5:7 GNB*

16) But if we claim to know him and don't obey him, we are lying and the truth isn't in our hearts. [5]**We truly love God only when we obey him as we should,** and then we know that we belong to him. [6]**If we say we are his, we must follow the example of Christ.** — *1 John 2:4-6 CEV*

17) Children, don't be fooled. Anyone who does right is good, just like Christ himself. — *1 John 3:7 CEV*

18) God's children cannot keep on being sinful. **His life-giving power lives in them and makes them** his children, so that they cannot keep on sinning. — *1 John 3:9 CEV*

9b) Living a Lifestyle That
Pleases The Lord

Read On: February 25th | May 12th | July 28th | October 13th | December 29th

1) "Did you notice my servant Job?" the LORD asked. "There is no one on earth as faithful and good as he is. **He worships me and is careful not to do anything evil.** You persuaded me to let you attack him for no reason at all, **but Job is still as faithful as ever.**" — *Job 2:3 GNB*

2) **If you will only obey me,** you will eat the **good things** the land produces. — *Isaiah 1:19 GNB*

3) **Your own sins will punish you, because it was a bitter mistake for you to reject me without fear of punishment.** I, the LORD All-Powerful, have spoken. — *Jeremiah 2:19 CEV*

4) The LORD said: People of Jerusalem, when you stumble and fall, you get back up, and if you take a wrong road, you turn round and go back. ⁵**So why do you refuse to come back to me? Why do you hold so tightly to your false gods?** ⁶**I listen carefully, but none of you admit that you've done wrong.** Without a second thought, you run down the wrong road like cavalry troops charging into battle. — *Jeremiah 8:4-6 CEV*

5) **My people, you love to wander away; you don't even try to stay close to me.** So now I will reject you and punish you for your sins. I, the LORD, have spoken. — *Jeremiah 14:10 CEV*

6) **My people, you abandoned me and walked away.** I am tired of showing mercy; that's why I'll destroy you. — *Jeremiah 15:6 CEV*

7) **They will no longer worship idols and do things that make them unacceptable to me. I will wash away their sin and make them clean,** and **I will protect them from everything that makes them unclean.** They will be my people, and I will be their God. — *Ezekiel 37:23 CEV*

8) But more than anything else, **put God's work first and do what he wants.** Then the other things **will be yours as well.** — *Matthew 6:33 CEV*

9) And he who sent me is with me; he has not left me alone, **because I always do what pleases him."** — *John 8:29 GNB*

10) So then, my brothers and sisters, because of God's great mercy to us I appeal to you: **offer yourselves as a living sacrifice to God, dedicated to his service and pleasing to him.** This is the true worship that you should offer. — *Romans 12:1 GNB*

11) **Work hard** and do **not be lazy.** Serve the Lord with a heart full of **devotion.** — *Romans 12:11 GNB*

12) Don't you know that **your body is the temple of the Holy Spirit,** who lives in you and who was given to you by God? **You do not belong to yourselves but to God.** — *1 Corinthians 6:19 GNB*

13) If we would **examine ourselves first,** we would not come under God's judgment. — *1 Corinthians 11:31 GNB*

14) God loves you and has chosen you as his own special people. **So be gentle, kind, humble, meek, and patient.** — *Colossians 3:12 CEV*

15) **Put up with each other,** and **forgive anyone who does you wrong,** just as Christ has forgiven you. — *Colossians 3:13 CEV*

16) **Your life must be controlled by love,** just as Christ loved us and gave his life for us as a sweet— smelling offering and sacrifice that pleases God. — *Ephesians 5:2 GNB*

17) That's also how it is with people. **The ones who stop doing evil and make themselves pure will become special.** Their lives will be holy and pleasing to their Master, and they will be able to do all kinds of good deeds. — *2 Timothy 2:21 CEV*

18) **Do your best to win full approval in God's sight,** as a worker who is not ashamed of his work, **one who correctly teaches the message of God's truth.**
— *2 Timothy 2:15 GNB*

19) All you young people should obey your elders. In fact, **everyone should be humble towards everyone else.** The Scriptures say, **"God opposes proud people, but he helps everyone who is humble."**
— *1 Peter 5:5 CEV*

20) The world and everything in it that people desire is passing away; **but those who do the will of God live forever.** — *1 John 2:17 GNB*

9c) Help Conquering
Your Bad Habits

Read On: February 26th | May 13th | July 29th | October 14th | December 30th

1) Remove my sin, and I will be clean; wash me, and I will be whiter than snow. — *Psalm 51:7 GNB*

2) Give me again the joy that comes from your salvation, and make me willing to obey you. — *Psalm 51:12 GNB*

3) Please help me learn to do the right thing, and I will be honest and fair in my own kingdom. ³I refuse to be corrupt or to take part in anything crooked, ⁴and I won't be dishonest or deceitful. — *Psalm 101:2-4 CEV*

4) Take away my foolish desires, and let me find life by walking with you. — *Psalm 119:37 CEV*

5) When you corrected me, it did me good because it taught me to study your laws. ⁷²I would rather obey you than to have a thousand pieces of silver and gold. — *Psalm 119:71-72 CEV*

6) Wash yourselves clean! I am disgusted with your filthy deeds. Stop doing wrong. — *Isaiah 1:16 CEV*

7) Our holy God lives forever in the highest heavens, and this is what he says: Though I live high above in the holy place, I am here to help those who are humble and depend only on me. — *Isaiah 57:15 CEV*

8) Do not let evil defeat you; instead, conquer evil with good. — *Romans 12:21 GNB*

9) The night is nearly over, day is almost here. Let us stop doing the things that belong to the dark, and let us take up weapons for fighting in the light. — *Romans 13:12 GNB*

10) Don't be immoral in matters of sex. That is a sin against your own body in a way that no other sin is. — *1 Corinthians 6:18 CEV*

11) Don't you know that **your body is the temple of the Holy Spirit, who lives in you and who was given to you by God?** You do not belong to yourselves but to God; ²⁰he bought you for a price. So use your bodies for God's glory. — *1 Corinthians 6:19-20 GNB*

12) My friends, God has made us these promises. **So we should stay away from everything that keeps our bodies and spirits from being clean.** We should honour God and try to be completely like him. — *2 Corinthians 7:1 CEV*

13) Actually all of us were like them **and lived according to our natural desires, doing whatever suited the wishes of our own bodies and minds.** In our natural condition we, like everyone else, were destined to suffer God's anger. — *Ephesians 2:3 GNB*

14) You were told that **your foolish desires will destroy you** and that **you must give up your old way of life with all its bad habits.** — *Ephesians 4:22 CEV*

15) Stop all your dirty talk. Say the right thing at the right time and help others by what you say. — *Ephesians 4:29 CEV*

16) Don't destroy yourself by getting drunk, but let the Spirit fill your life. — *Ephesians 5:18 CEV*

18) Such a large crowd of witnesses is all around us! **So we must get rid of everything that slows us down, especially the sin that just won't let go.** And we must be determined to run the race that is ahead of us. — *Hebrews 12:1 CEV*

17) And stop lying to each other. You have given up **your old way of life with its habits.** — *Colossians 3:9 CEV*

19) So get rid of every filthy habit and all wicked conduct. Submit to God and accept the word that he plants in your hearts, which is able to save you. — *James 1:21 GNB*

20) Rid yourselves, then, of all evil; no more **lying** or **hypocrisy** or **jealousy** or **insulting language.** — *1 Peter 2:1 GNB*

9d) Learning to Live a
Pure and Holy Lifestyle

Read On: February 27th | May 14th | July 30th | October 15th | December 31st

1) If you obey my laws and teachings, you will live safely in the land **and enjoy its abundant crops.** — *Leviticus 25:18-19 CEV*

2) The Lord your God commands you to love him and to serve him with all your heart and soul. If you obey him. — *Deuteronomy 11:13 CEV*

3) If you obey these laws, you will be doing what the Lord your God says is right and good. Then **he will help you** and your descendants **be successful.** — *Deuteronomy 12:28 CEV*

4) "Tell me," Samuel said. "Does the LORD really want sacrifices and offerings? No! He doesn't want your sacrifices. **He wants you to obey him.** — *1 Samuel 15:22 CEV*

5) I want to obey your commands; give me new life, for you are righteous. — *Psalm 119:40 GNB*

6) Do not be conformed to this world (this age), [fashioned after and adapted to its external, superficial customs], but be transformed (changed) by the [entire] renewal of your mind [by its new ideals and its new attitude], so that you may prove [for yourselves] what is the good and acceptable and perfect will of God, even the thing which is good and acceptable and perfect [in His sight for you]. — *Romans 12:2 AMP*

7) Be sincere in your love for others. Hate everything that is evil and hold tight to everything that is good. ¹⁰Love each other as brothers and sisters and **honour others more than you do yourself.** — *Romans 12:9-10 CEV*

8) Share your belongings with your needy fellow Christians, and open your homes to strangers. — *Romans 12:13 GNB*

9) If someone has done you wrong, do not repay him with a wrong. Try to do what everyone considers to be good. — *Romans 12:17 GNB*

10) Therefore if any person is [ingrafted] in Christ (the Messiah) he is a new creation (a new creature altogether); the old [previous moral and spiritual condition] has passed away. Behold, the fresh and new has come! — *2 Corinthians 5:17 AMP*

11) So, come out from among [unbelievers], and separate (sever) yourselves from them, says the Lord, and touch not [any] unclean thing; then I will receive you kindly and treat you with favor. — *2 Corinthians 6:17 AMP*

12) Let the Spirit change your way of thinking 24and make you into a new person. You were created to be like God, and so you must please him and be truly holy. — *Ephesians 4:23 – 24 CEV*

13) Instead, be kind and tender-hearted to one another, and forgive one another, as God has forgiven you through Christ. — *Ephesians 4:32 GNB*

14) Since you are God's dear children, you must try to be like him. — *Ephesians 5:1 GNB*

15) Let this same attitude and purpose and [humble] mind be in you which was in Christ Jesus: [Let Him be your example in humility:] — *Philippians 2:5 AMP*

16) Let us be concerned for one another, to help one another to show love and to do good. — *Hebrews 10:24 GNB*

17) Keep your lives free from the love of money, and be satisfied with what you have. For God has said, "I will never leave you; I will never abandon you." — *Hebrews 13:5 GNB*

18) Our foolish pride comes from this world, and so do our selfish desires and our desire to have everything we see. None of this comes from the Father. — *1 John 2:16 CEV*

19) You know that Christ is righteous; you should know, then, that everyone who does what is right is God's child. — *1 John 2:29 GNB*

20) Everyone who has this hope in Christ keeps himself pure, just as Christ is pure. — *1 John 3:3 GNB*

21) Little children, you are of God [you belong to Him] and have [already] defeated and overcome them [the agents of the antichrist], because He Who lives in you is greater (mightier) than he who is in the world. — *1 John 4:4 AMP*

9e) Making Positive Changes to Your Lifestyle

Read On: February 28th | May 15th | July 31st | October 16th

1) That's why the LORD our God **demands that we obey his laws and worship him** with fear and trembling. **And if we do, he will protect us and help us be successful.** — *Deuteronomy 6:24-25 CEV*

2) he said, "Always remember this song I have taught you today. **And let it be a warning that you must teach your children to obey everything written in** The Book of God's Law. — *Deuteronomy 32:46 CEV*

3) Rebelling against God or disobeying him because you are proud **is just as bad as worshiping idols** or asking them for advice. **You refused to do what God told you,** so God has decided that you can't be king." — *1 Samuel 15:23 CEV*

4) LORD, who may enter your Temple? Who may worship on Zion, your sacred hill? ²**Those who obey God in everything and always do what is right,** whose words are true and sincere. -*Psalm 15:1-2 GNB*

5) I want to obey your commands; give me new life, for you are righteous. — *Psalm 119:40 GNB*

6) You, Lord, are my choice, and I will obey you. ⁵⁸With all my heart I beg you to be kind to me, just as you have promised. ⁵⁹**I pay careful attention as you lead me, and I follow closely.** — *Psalm 119:57-59 CEV*

7) I won't ever forget your teachings, **because you give me new life by following them.** — *Psalm 119:93 CEV*

8) Those who do not **take up their cross and follow in my steps** are not fit **to be my disciples.** — *Matthew 10:38 GNB*

9) You must love him with all your heart, soul, mind, and **strength.**' — *Mark 12:30 CEV*

10) Whoever is faithful in small matters will be faithful in large ones; whoever is dishonest in small matters will be dishonest in large ones. — *Luke 16:10 GNB*

163

Scripture Therapy Daily Devotional For Men

11) Stay joined to me and let my teachings become part of you. Then you can pray for whatever you want, and your prayer will be answered. — *John 15:7 CEV*

12) Only those people who are led by God's Spirit are his children. — *Romans 8:14 CEV*

13) And so, each of us must give an account to God for what we do. — *Romans 14:12 CEV*

14) I may be able to speak the languages of human beings and even of angels, but if I have no love, my speech is no more than a noisy gong or a clanging bell. — *1 Corinthians 13:1 GNB*

15) What if I could prophesy and understand all secrets and all knowledge? And what if I had faith that moved mountains? I would be nothing, unless I loved others. — *1 Corinthians 13:2 CEV*

16) Keep on being faithful to what you were taught and to what you believed. After all, you know who taught you these things. — *2 Timothy 3:14 CEV*

17) and you remember that ever since you were a child, you have known the Holy Scriptures, which are able to give you the wisdom that leads to salvation through faith in Christ Jesus. — *2 Timothy 3:15 GNB*

18) Everything in the Scriptures is God's Word. All of it is useful for teaching and helping people and for correcting them and showing them how to live. ¹⁷The Scriptures train God's servants to do all kinds of good deeds. — *2 Timothy 3:16-17 CEV*

19) In the same way instruct the older women to behave as women should who live a holy life. They must not be slanderers or slaves to wine. They must teach what is good. — *Titus 2:3 GNB*

20) So keep your mind on Jesus, who put up with many insults from sinners. Then you won't get discouraged and give up. — *Hebrews 12:3 CEV*

21) Do not deceive yourselves by just listening to his word; instead, put it into practice. — *James 1:22 GNB*

22) But you, my friends, keep on building yourselves up on your most sacred faith. Pray in the power of the Holy Spirit. — *Jude 1:20 GNB*

CHAPTER 10

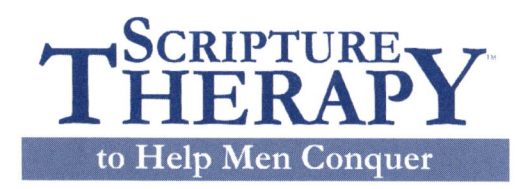

Scripture Therapy™ to Help Men Conquer
Attitude Issues

TOPICS

10a) Keeping a Positive Attitude at All Times
Read On: February 29th | May 16th | August 1st | October 17th

10b) Showing Kindness and Humility in Your Attitude
Read On: March 1st | May 17th | August 2nd | October 18th

10c) Changing Negative Parts of Your Attitude
Read On: March 2nd | May 18th | August 3rd | October 19th

10d) Developing a Christ-Like Attitude
Read On: March 3rd | May 19th | August 4th | October 20th

10e) Having a Good Attitude Towards Life
Read On: March 4th | May 20th | August 5th | October 21st

10f) Controlling Your Attitude When Angry
Read On: March 5th | May 21st | August 6th | October 22nd

10a) Keeping a Positive
Attitude at All Times

Read On: February 29th | May 16th | August 1st | October 17th

1) So I'll **make you wiser than anyone who has ever lived** or ever will live. — *1 Kings 3:12 CEV*

2) Hear me, LORD, and be merciful! Help me, LORD!" ¹¹You have changed my sadness into a joyful dance; you have taken away my sorrow and surrounded me with joy. ¹²So I will not be silent; I will sing praise to you. LORD, you are my God, I will give you thanks forever. — *Psalm 30:10-12 GNB*

3) Give yourself to the LORD; trust in him, and **he will help you;** — *Psalm 37:5 GNB*

4) Don't ever think that you are wise enough, **but respect the Lord and stay away from evil.** — *Proverbs 3:7 CEV*

5) Be careful how you think; your life is shaped by your **thoughts.** — *Proverbs 4:23 GNB*

6) You can **persuade others** if you are wise and **speak sensibly.** — *Proverbs 16:23 CEV*

7) Watching what you say can save you a lot of trouble. — *Proverbs 21:23 CEV*

8) Fear not [there is nothing to fear], **for I am with you; do not look around you in terror** and **be dismayed,** for I am your God. **I will strengthen** and **harden** you to difficulties, yes, **I will help you;** yes, I will **hold you up** and **retain you with My [victorious] right hand** of rightness and justice. — *Isaiah 41:10 AMP*

9) Can any of you **live a bit longer by worrying about it?** — *Matthew 6:27 GNB*

10) "So do not start worrying: 'Where will my food come from? or my drink? or my clothes?' ³²(These are the things the pagans are always concerned about.) Your Father in heaven knows that you need all these things. ³³Instead, be concerned above everything else with the Kingdom of God and with what he requires of you, and he will provide you with all these other things. — *Matthew 6:31-33 GNB*

11) Keep watch and pray that you will not fall into temptation. **The spirit is willing, but the flesh is weak.**" — *Matthew 26:41 GNB*

Scripture Therapy Daily Devotional For Men

12) And Jesus, replying, said to them, **Have faith in God [constantly].** — *Mark 11:22 AMP*

13) Truly I tell you, whoever says to this mountain, Be lifted up and thrown into the sea! **and does not doubt at all in his heart but believes that what he says will take place, it will be done for him.** — *Mark 11:23 AMP*

14) For this reason I am telling you, whatever you ask for in prayer, **believe (trust and be confident) that it is granted to you, and you will [get it].** — *Mark 11:24 AMP*

15) For with God nothing is ever impossible and no **word from God** shall be without **power** or impossible of **fulfillment.** — *Luke 1:37 AMP*

16) The Spirit has given us life; **he must also control our lives.** — *Galatians 5:25 GNB*

17) So let us not become tired of doing good; for if we do not give up, the time will come when we will reap the **harvest.** — *Galatians 6:9 GNB*

18) I ask the glorious Father and God of our Lord Jesus Christ **to give you his Spirit. The Spirit will make you wise and let you understand what it means to know God.** — *Ephesians 1:17 CEV*

19) May you be made **strong** with all the strength which comes from his glorious power, **so that you may be able to endure everything with patience. And with joy give thanks to the Father,** who has made you fit to have your share of what God has reserved for his people in the kingdom of light. — *Colossians 1:11-12 GNB*

20) Do not lose your courage, then, because it brings with it **a great reward.** — *Hebrews 10:35 GNB*

21) Learn to be patient, so that you will **please God** and be given what he has promised. — *Hebrews 10:36 CEV*

22) If any of you need wisdom, you should ask God, and it will be given to you. God is generous and won't correct you for asking. — *James 1:5 CEV*

23) God cares for you, **so turn all your worries over to him.**
— *1 Peter 5:7 CEV*

24) Are any of you wise or sensible? **Then show it by living right and by being humble and wise in everything you do.**
— *James 3:13 CEV*

10b) Showing Kindness and Humility In Your Attitude

Read On: March 1st | May 17th | August 2nd | October 18th

1) Moses was a **humble man**, more humble **than anyone else on earth.** — *Numbers 12:3 GNB*

2) Kind words are like honey — they **cheer you up** and make you **feel strong.** — *Proverbs 16:24 CEV*

3) She **speaks** with a **gentle wisdom.** — *Proverbs 31:26 GNB*

4) Whoever exalts himself [with haughtiness and empty pride] shall be humbled (brought low), and whoever humbles himself [whoever has a modest opinion of himself and behaves accordingly] shall be raised to honor. — *Matthew 23:12 AMP*

5) Treat others **just as you want to be treated.** — *Luke 6:31 CEV*

6) Be friendly with everyone. Don't be proud and feel that you are cleverer than others. Make friends with ordinary people. — *Romans 12:16 CEV*

7) You should each judge your own conduct. If it is good, then you can be proud of what you yourself have done, without having to compare it with what someone else has done. — *Galatians 6:4 GNB*

8) And be constantly renewed in the spirit of your mind [having a fresh mental and spiritual attitude]. — *Ephesians 4:23 AMP*

9) And **become useful** and **helpful** and **kind** to one another, **tenderhearted** (compassionate, understanding, loving— hearted), forgiving one another [readily and freely], as God in Christ **forgave you.** — *Ephesians 4:32 AMP*

10) Don't do anything from selfish ambition or from a cheap desire to boast, but be humble towards one another, always considering others better than yourselves. ⁴And look out for one another's interests, not just for your own. — *Philippians 2:3– 4 GNB*

11) But now you must stop doing such things. **You must stop being angry, hateful, and evil. You must no longer say insulting or cruel things about others.** — *Colossians 3:8 CEV*

12) Each of you is now a new person. You are becoming more and more **like your Creator,** and you will understand him better. — *Colossians 3:10 CEV*

13) That's also how it is with people. **The ones who stop doing evil and make themselves pure will become special.** Their lives will be holy and pleasing to their Master, **and they will be able to do all kinds of good deeds.** — *2 Timothy 2:21 CEV*

14) Instead, in order that none of you be deceived by sin and become stubborn, **you must help one another every day, as long as the word "Today" in the scripture applies to us.** — *Hebrews 3:13 GNB*

15) We do not want you to become lazy, **but to be like those who believe and are patient, and so receive what God has promised.** — *Hebrews 6:12 GNB*

16) Try to be at peace with everyone, and try to live a holy life, because no one will see the Lord without it. — *Hebrews 12:14 GNB*

17) Are any of you wise or sensible? **Then show it by living right and by being humble and wise in everything you do.** — *James 3:13 CEV*

18) To conclude: **you must all have the same attitude** and the same **feelings;** love one another as brothers and sisters, and be kind and humble with one another. — *1 Peter 3:8 GNB*

19) They must turn away from evil and do good; they must **strive for peace** with all their heart. — *1 Peter 3:11 GNB*

20) Therefore humble yourselves [demote, lower yourselves in your own estimation] under the mighty hand of God, that in due time He may exalt you. — *1 Peter 5:6 AMP*

10c) Changing Negative Parts of Your Attitude

Read On: March 2nd | May 18th | August 3rd | October 19th

1) "Tell me," Samuel said. "Does the LORD really want sacrifices and offerings? **No! He doesn't want your sacrifices. He wants you to obey him.** — *1 Samuel 15:22 CEV*

2) Give me the desire to obey **your laws** rather than to get rich. — *Psalm 119:36 GNB*

3) **You, LORD,** are my choice, and **I will obey you.** — *Psalm 119:57 CEV*

4) How long is the lazy man going to lie in bed? When is he ever going to get up? ¹⁰"I'll just take a short nap," he says; "I'll fold my hands and rest a while." ¹¹But while he sleeps, **poverty will attack him like an armed robber.** — *Proverbs 6:9-11 GNB*

5) There are six or seven kinds of people the LORD doesn't like: ¹⁷Those who are too **proud** or **tell lies** or **murder,** ¹⁸those who make evil plans or are quick to do wrong, ¹⁹those who **tell lies in court** or stir up **trouble** in a **family.** — *Proverbs 6:16-19 CEV*

6) Obey the teaching of your **parents.** — *Proverbs 6:20 CEV*

7) I always **speak the truth** and **refuse to tell a lie.** — *Proverbs 8:7 CEV*

8) **Too much pride can put you to shame.** It's wiser to be humble. — *Proverbs 11:2 CEV*

9) Fools **think they know** what is best, **but a sensible person listens to advice.** — *Proverbs 12:15 CEV*

10) All who refuse correction will be poor and disgraced; all who **accept correction will be praised.** — *Proverbs 13:18 CEV*

11) Obey the Lord's teachings and you will live — disobey and you will die. — *Proverbs 19:16 CEV*

12) **Wicked people** are controlled by their conceit and **arrogance, and this is sinful.** — *Proverbs 21:4 GNB*

14) Everyone must obey **state authorities,** because no authority exists **without God's** permission, and the existing authorities have been put there by God. ²Whoever opposes the existing authority **opposes what God has ordered;** and **anyone who does so will bring judgment on himself.** — *Romans 13:1-2 GNB*

17) My friends, you were chosen to be free. **So don't use your freedom as an excuse to do anything you want.** Use it as an opportunity to serve each other with love. — *Galatians 5:13 CEV*

13) Anyone who can be trusted in little matters can also be trusted in important matters. **But anyone who is dishonest in little matters will be dishonest in important matters.** — *Luke 16:10 CEV*

15) For this reason you must **obey the authorities** — not just because of God's punishment, but also **as a matter of conscience.** — *Romans 13:5 GNB*

16) You are tempted in the same way that everyone else is tempted. **But God can be trusted not to let you be tempted too much, and he will show you how to escape from your temptations.** — *1 Corinthians 10:13 CEV*

18) **Don't use dirty** or **foolish** or **filthy words.** Instead, say how thankful you are. — *Ephesians 5:4 CEV*

19) Such a large crowd of witnesses is all around us! **So we must get rid of everything that slows us down, especially the sin that just won't let go.** And we must be determined to run the race that is ahead of us. — *Hebrews 12:1 CEV*

20) So then, **submit to God.** Resist the Devil, and he will run away **from you.** — *James 4:7 GNB*

10d) Developing
A Christ-Like Attitude

Read On: March 3rd | May 19th | August 4th | October 20th

1) That's why **the LORD our God demands that we obey his laws** and **worship him with fear and trembling**. And if we do, he will **protect us** and **help us be successful**. — *Deuteronomy 6:24-25 CEV*

2) This Book of the Law **shall not depart out of your mouth,** but you shall **meditate on it day and night,** that you may **observe** and **do** according to all that is written in it. For then you shall **make your way prosperous,** and then you shall **deal wisely** and **have good success.** — *Joshua 1:8 AMP*

3) Instead, I told them, "If you listen to me and do what I tell you, I will be your God, you will be my people, and all will go well for you." — *Jeremiah 7:23 CEV*

4) But I tell you to **love your enemies** and **pray for anyone who ill-treats you.** — *Matthew 5:44 CEV*

5) Anyone who comes and listens to me and obeys me [48]is like someone who **dug down deep and built a house on solid rock.** When the flood came and the river rushed against the house, **it was built so well that it didn't even shake.** — *Luke 6:47-48 CEV*

6) Jesus said to his disciples **If you love me, you will do as I command.** — *John 14:15 CEV*

7) But anyone who doesn't love me, won't obey me. What they have heard me say doesn't really come from me, **but from the Father who sent me.** — *John 14:24 CEV*

8) If you obey me, I will keep loving you, just as my Father keeps loving me, because I have obeyed him. — *John 15:10 CEV*

9) So **I command** you to **love each other.** — *John 15:17 CEV*

10) **God accepts those who obey his Law,** but not those who simply hear it. — *Romans 2:13 CEV*

11) **Love one another warmly as Christian brothers and sisters,** and be eager to show **respect** for one another. — *Romans 12:10 GNB*

12) If someone has done you wrong, **do not repay him with a wrong.** Try to do what everyone considers to be good. ¹⁸**Do everything possible on your part to live in peace with everybody.** — *Romans 12:17-18 GNB*

13) **It is love, then, that you should strive for.** Set your hearts on spiritual gifts, especially the gift of **proclaiming God's message.** — *1 Corinthians 14:1 GNB*

14) **Love should always make us tell the truth.** Then we will grow in every way and be more like Christ, the head. — *Ephesians 4:15 CEV*

15) and you must **put on the new self, which is created in God's likeness** and reveals itself in the true life that is upright and holy. — *Ephesians 4:24 GNB*

16) Now, the important thing is that **your way of life should be as the gospel of Christ requires,** so that, whether or not I am able to go and see you, **I will hear that you are standing firm** with one common purpose and that with only one desire **you are fighting together for the faith of the gospel.** — *Philippians 1:27 GNB*

17) **The attitude you should have** is the one that Christ Jesus had. — *Philippians 2:5 GNB*

18) So then, dear friends, **as you always obeyed me** when I was with you, **it is even more important that you obey me now while I am away from you.** Keep on working with fear and trembling to complete your salvation. — *Philippians 2:12 GNB*

19) Then you will be able to live as the Lord wants and will always do what pleases him. Your lives will produce all kinds of **good deeds,** and you will **grow** in your **knowledge of God.** — *Colossians 1:10 GNB*

20) My brothers and sisters, as believers in our Lord Jesus Christ, the Lord of glory, **you must never treat people in different ways according to their outward appearance.**
— *James 2:1 GNB*

21) **All you young people should obey your elders. In fact, everyone should be humble towards everyone else.** The Scriptures say, "God opposes proud people, but he helps everyone who is humble."
— *1 Peter 5:5 CEV*

22) My dear friends, **we are now God's children,** but it is not yet clear what we shall become. **But we know that when Christ appears, we shall be like him,** because we shall see him as he really is. ³**Everyone who has this hope in Christ keeps himself pure, just as Christ is pure.** — *1 John 3:2-3 GNB*

10e) Having a Good
Attitude Towards Life

Read On: March 4th | May 20th | August 5th | October 21st

1) **The lifestyle of good people** is like sunlight at dawn that keeps getting **brighter** until broad daylight. — *Proverbs 4:18 CEV*

2) **Being lazy will make you poor,** but hard work will make you rich. — *Proverbs 10:4 GNB*

3) Giving the **right answer** at the **right time** makes everyone **happy.** — *Proverbs 15:23 CEV*

4) **Show me someone who does a good job,** and I will show you someone who is **better than most** and worthy of the company of kings. — *Proverbs 22:29 GNB*

5) **Our holy God lives forever in the highest heavens,** and this is what he says: Though I live high above in the holy place, **I am here to help those who are humble and depend only on me.** — *Isaiah 57:15 CEV*

6) **Do not be conformed to this world (this age),** [fashioned after and adapted to its external, superficial customs], **but be transformed (changed) by the [entire] renewal of your mind [by its new ideals and its new attitude],** so that you may prove [for yourselves] what is the good and acceptable and perfect will of God, even the thing which is good and acceptable and perfect **[in His sight for you].** — *Romans 12:2 AMP*

7) And because of God's gracious gift to me I say to every one of you: **do not think of yourself more highly than you should.** Instead, be **modest in your thinking,** and judge yourself according to the amount of faith that God has given you. — *Romans 12:3 GNB*

8) **God is the one who makes us patient and cheerful.** I pray that **he will help you live at peace with each other, as you follow Christ.** — *Romans 15:5 CEV*

Scripture Therapy Daily Devotional For Men

9) Try your best to let God's Spirit **keep your hearts united. Do this by living at peace.** — *Ephesians 4:3 CEV*

10) Finally, my friends, **keep your minds** on whatever is true, pure, right, holy, friendly, and proper. **Don't ever stop thinking about what is truly worthwhile and worthy of praise.** — *Philippians 4:8 CEV*

11) God loves you and has chosen you as his own special people. **So be gentle, kind, humble, meek, and patient.** — *Colossians 3:12 CEV*

12) Put up with each other, and **forgive anyone who does you wrong,** just as Christ has forgiven you. — *Colossians 3:13 CEV*

13) Don't let anyone forget these things. And with God as your witness, you must warn them not to argue about words. **These arguments don't help anyone. In fact, they ruin everyone who listens to them.** — *2 Timothy 2:14 CEV*

14) Remind your people to obey the rulers and authorities and not to be rebellious. They must always be ready to do something helpful. — *Titus 3:1 CEV*

15) Obey your leaders and do what they say. They are watching over you, and **they must answer to God.** So don't make them sad as they do their work. **Make them happy. Otherwise, they won't be able to help you at all.** — *Hebrews 13:17 CEV*

16) If you don't do what you know is right, you have sinned. — *James 4:17 CEV*

17) Behave like obedient children. **Don't let your lives be controlled by your desires, as they used to be.** — *1 Peter 1:14 CEV*

18) But if we claim to know him and don't obey him, we are lying and the truth isn't in our hearts. — *1 John 2:4 CEV*

19) We truly love God only when we obey him as we should, and then we know that we belong to him. — *1 John 2:5 CEV*

10f) Controlling
Your Attitude When Angry

Read On: March 5th | May 21st | August 6th | October 22nd

1) To worry yourself to death with resentment would be a **foolish, senseless** thing to do. — *Job 5:2 GNB*

2) When people are happy, they **smile,** but when they are **sad,** they look **depressed.** — *Proverbs 15:13 GNB*

3) You will have to live **with the consequences** of **everything** you say. — *Proverbs 18:20 GNB*

4) What you say can preserve life or destroy it; so you must accept the **consequences** of your **words.** — *Proverbs 18:21 GNB*

5) And whenever you stand praying, **if you have anything against anyone, forgive him** and **let it drop (leave it, let it go),** in order that your Father Who is in heaven **may also forgive you your** [own] **failings** and **shortcomings** and **let them drop.** — *Mark 11:25 AMP*

6) My dear friends, as a follower of our Lord Jesus Christ, **I beg you to get along with each other. Don't take sides. Always try to agree in what you think.** — *1 Corinthians 1:10 CEV*

7) **love is not ill— mannered** or **selfish** or **irritable; love does not keep a record of wrongs.** — *1 Corinthians 13:5 GNB*

8) Do not use **harmful words,** but only **helpful words,** the kind that **build up** and **provide what is needed,** so that **what** you say will do good to those who **hear** you. — *Ephesians 4:29 GNB*

9) Get rid of all **bitterness, passion,** and **anger.** No more **shouting** or **insults,** no more **hateful feelings** of any sort. — *Ephesians 4:31 GNB*

10) Instead, be **kind** and **tender-hearted** to one another, and **forgive one another,** as God has **forgiven you** through **Christ.** — *Ephesians 4:32 GNB*

11) **Children, you belong to the Lord, and you do the right thing when you obey your parents.** The first commandment with a promise says, ²**Obey your father and your mother,** ³**and you will have a long and happy life."** — *Ephesians 6:1-3 CEV*

12) Your speech should always be **pleasant and interesting,** and you should know how to give the right answer to everyone.
— *Colossians 4:6 GNB*

13) Church officials **must be in control** of their own families, **and they must see that their children are obedient and always respectful.**
— *1 Timothy 3:4 CEV*

14) they must have a good reputation and be faithful in marriage. Their **children must be followers of the Lord** and not have a reputation **for being wild and disobedient.** — *Titus 1:6 CEV*

15) Make sure that no one misses out on God's wonderful kindness. Don't let anyone become **bitter** and **cause trouble** for the rest of you. — *Hebrews 12:15 CEV*

16) Do not deceive yourselves **by just listening to his word;** instead, **put it into practice.** — *James 1:22 GNB*

17) If you think you are being religious, **but can't control your tongue, you are fooling yourself,** and everything you do is useless. — *James 1:26 CEV*

18) And the tongue is **like a fire.** It is a world of wrong, occupying its place in our bodies and spreading evil through our whole being. **It sets on fire the entire course of our existence with the fire that comes to it from hell itself.**
— *James 3:6 GNB*

19) My dear friends, **with our tongues** we speak both praises and curses. **We praise our Lord and Father, and we curse people who were created to be like God, and this isn't right.** — *James 3:9-10 CEV*

CHAPTER 11

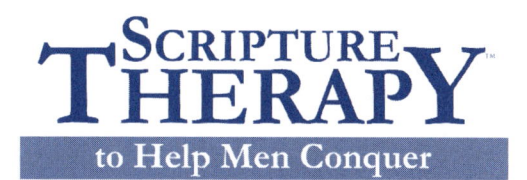

SCRIPTURE THERAPY™
to Help Men Conquer
SPIRITUAL GROWTH ISSUES

TOPICS

11a) Confidence in The Power of Your Prayers
Read On: March 6th | May 22nd | August 7th | October 23rd

11b) Obeying The Lord With All Your Heart
Read On: March 7th | May 23rd | August 8th | October 24th

11c) Being Faithful to Obey God's Commands
Read On: March 8th | May 24th | August 9th | October 25th

11d) Getting Sin Out of Your Lifestyle
Read On: March 9th | May 25th | August 10th | October 26th

11e) Having Faith and Trust in The Lord
Read On: March 10th | May 26th | August 11th | October 27th

11f) Being Faithful to Worship The Lord Daily
Read On: March 11th | May 27th | August 12th | October 28th

11g) Victory Over The Power of Your Enemy
Read On: March 12th | May 28th | August 13th | October 29th

11a) Confidence in The Power of
Your Prayers

Read On: March 6th | May 22nd | August 7th | October 23rd

1) **I pray to you, God, because you will help me.** Listen and answer my prayer! — *Psalm 17:6 CEV*

2) Everyone will come to you **because you answer prayer.** — *Psalm 65:2 CEV*

3) Let's praise God! **He listened when I prayed, and he is always kind.** — *Psalm 66:20 CEV*

5) If you have faith when you pray, you will be given whatever you ask for." — *Matthew 21:22 CEV*

4) Ask the LORD to bless your plans, and you will be successful in carrying them out. — *Proverbs 16:3 GNB*

7) For everyone who asks and keeps on asking receives; and he who **seeks and keeps on seeking finds**; and to him who **knocks and keeps on knocking,** the door shall be opened. — *Luke 11:10 AMP*

6) For this reason I am telling you, **whatever you ask for in prayer,** believe **(trust and be confident) that it is granted to you,** and you will **[get it]**. — *Mark 11:24 AMP*

8) Jesus told his disciples a story about **how they should keep on praying and never give up:** — *Luke 18:1 CEV*

9) Ask me, and I will do whatever you ask. This way the Son will bring honour to the Father. — *John 14:13 CEV*

10) In the same way the **Spirit** also **comes to help us,** weak as we are. For we do not know how **we ought** to pray; **the Spirit himself pleads with God for us** in groans that words cannot express. — *Romans 8:26 GNB*

11) And **God, who sees into our hearts,** knows **what the thought of the Spirit is;** because the Spirit **pleads with God on behalf of his people** and **in accordance with his will.** — *Romans 8:27 GNB*

Scripture Therapy Daily Devotional For Men

12) Let your hope make you glad. **Be patient in time of trouble** and **never stop praying.** — *Romans 12:12 CEV*

13) To him who by means of his power working in us is able to do so much more than we can ever **ask for**, or even **think of.** — *Ephesians 3:20 GNB*

14) Do not fret or have any anxiety about anything, but in every circumstance and in everything, **by prayer and petition (definite requests), with thanksgiving, continue to make your wants known to God.** — *Philippians 4:6 AMP*

15) Never give up praying. And when you **pray,** keep alert and **be thankful.** — *Colossians 4:2 CEV*

16) First of all, **I ask you to pray for everyone.** Ask God to help and bless them all, and **tell God how thankful you are for each of them.** — *1 Timothy 2:1 CEV*

17) So whenever we are in need, we should **come bravely before the throne of our merciful God.** There we will be treated with undeserved kindness, and **we will find help.** — *Hebrews 4:16 CEV*

18) But **without faith** no one can **please God.** We must **believe that God is real** and that **he rewards everyone** who **searches** for him. — *Hebrews 11:6 CEV*

19) If any of you need wisdom, you should ask God, and **it will be given to you.** God is generous and won't correct you for asking. — *James 1:5 CEV*

20) But when you pray, you must believe and not doubt at all. Whoever doubts is like a wave in the sea that is driven and blown about by the wind. [7]**People like that, unable to make up their minds** and undecided in all they do, must not think that they will receive anything from the L<small>ORD</small>. — *James 1:6-8 GNB*

183

21) If you have sinned, **you should tell each other what you have done.** Then you can pray for one another and be healed. **The prayer of an innocent person is powerful, and it can help a lot.**
— *James 5:16 CEV*

22) **The Lord watches over everyone who obeys him, and he listens to their prayers.** But he opposes everyone who does evil." — *1 Peter 3:12 CEV*

23) God cares for you, **so turn all your worries over to him.** — *1 Peter 5:7 CEV*

11b) Obeying The Lord
With All Your Heart

Read On: March 7th | May 23rd | August 8th | October 24th

1) **Dedicate yourselves to me** and **be holy** because I am the LORD your God. — *Leviticus 20:7 CEV*

2) I have chosen you as my people, **and I expect you to obey my laws.** — *Leviticus 20:8 CEV*

3) Everything Hezekiah did while he was king of Judah, including what he did for the temple in Jerusalem, **was right and good. He was a successful king, because he obeyed the LORD God with all his heart.** — *2 Chronicles 31:20-21 CEV*

4) LORD God of heaven, you are great and fearsome. **And you faithfully keep your promises to everyone who loves you and obeys your commands.** — *Nehemiah 1:5 CEV*

5) The lifestyle of good people is like sunlight at dawn that keeps getting brighter until broad daylight. — *Proverbs 4:18 CEV*

6) Those who have reverence for the Lord will learn from him the path they should **follow.** [13]They will **always be prosperous, and their children will possess the land.** [14]The LORD is the friend of those who obey him and he affirms his covenant with them. — *Psalm 25:12-14 GNB*

7) Happy are those whose greatest desire is to do what God requires; God will satisfy them fully! — *Matthew 5:6 GNB*

8) But I tell you to love your enemies and pray for anyone who ill-treats you. — *Matthew 5:44 CEV*

10) If you **confess that Jesus is Lord** and **believe** that God raised him from death, you will be saved. — *Romans 10:9 GNB*

9) I give you a new commandment: that you should love one another. Just as I have loved you, so you too should love one another. — *John 13:34 AMP*

185

Scripture Therapy Daily Devotional For Men

11) Love one another warmly as Christian brothers and sisters, and be eager to show respect for one another. — *Romans 12:10 GNB*

12) Bless those who persecute you [who are cruel in their attitude toward you]; bless and do not curse them. — *Romans 12:14 AMP*

13) My dear friends, as a follower of our Lord Jesus Christ, I beg you to get along with each other. Don't take sides. Always try to agree in what you think. — *1 Corinthians 1:10 CEV*

14) I harden my body with blows and bring it under complete control, to keep myself from being disqualified after having called others to the contest. — *1 Corinthians 9:27 GNB*

15) Show love in everything you do. — *1 Corinthians 16:14 CEV*

16) May Christ through your faith [actually] dwell (settle down, abide, make His permanent home) in your hearts! May you be rooted deep in love and founded securely on love. — *Ephesians 3:17 AMP*

17) Let the Spirit change your way of thinking [24] and make you into a new person. You were created to be like God, and so you must please him and be truly holy. — *Ephesians 4:23-24 CEV*

18) And I am convinced and sure of this very thing, that He Who began a good work in you will continue until the day of Jesus Christ [right up to the time of His return], developing [that good work] and perfecting and bringing it to full completion in you. — *Philippians 1:6 AMP*

19) God loves you and has chosen you as his own special people. So be gentle, kind, humble, meek, and patient. — *Colossians 3:12 CEV*

20) Put up with each other, and forgive anyone who does you wrong, just as Christ has forgiven you. — *Colossians 3:13 CEV*

21) Your speech should always be pleasant and interesting, and you should know how to give the right answer to everyone. — *Colossians 4:6 GNB*

11c) Being Faithful to
Obey God's Commands

Read On: March 8th | May 24th | August 9th | October 25th

1) You know that the LORD your God is the only true God. **So love him and obey his commands, and he will faithfully keep his agreement with you and your descendants** for a thousand generations. — *Deuteronomy 7:9 CEV*

2) If you completely obey these laws, the Lord your **God will be loyal and keep the agreement he made with you,** just as he promised our ancestors. — *Deuteronomy 7:12 CEV*

3) People of Israel, what does the LORD your God want from you? **The LORD wants you to respect and follow him, to love and serve him with all your heart and soul.** — *Deuteronomy 10:12 CEV*

4) Moses taught you to love the LORD your God, to be faithful to him, and to worship and obey him with your whole heart and with all your strength. So be very careful to do everything Moses commanded. — *Joshua 22:5 CEV*

5) **Be sure to love the LORD your God always.** — *Joshua 23:11 CEV*

6) **You will show me the path that leads to life;** your presence fills me with joy and brings me pleasure forever. — *Psalm 16:11 GNB*

7) **Your laws** are my greatest joy! **I follow their advice.** — *Psalm 119:24 CEV*

9) **Learn what I teach you, my son,** and **never forget what I tell you to do.** — *Proverbs 2:1 GNB*

8) Your **word** is a **lamp to guide me and a light for my path.** — *Psalm 119:105 GNB*

10) **Pay attention to what I say, my son. Listen to my words.** 21**Never let them get away from you. Remember them and keep them in your heart.** 22**They will give life** and **health** to anyone who understands them. — *Proverbs 4:20-22 GNB*

Scripture Therapy Daily Devotional For Men

11) There are many who say, "You can trust me!" **But can they be trusted?** — *Proverbs 20:6 CEV*

12) Jesus drew near and said to them, "I have been given all authority in heaven and on earth. ¹⁹**Go, then, to all peoples everywhere and make them my disciples:** baptize them in the name of the Father, the Son, and the Holy Spirit, ²⁰and teach them to obey everything I have commanded you. And I will be with you always, to the end of the age." — *Matthew 28:18-20 GNB*

13) If you [really] love Me, you will keep (obey) My commands. — *John 14:15 AMP*

14) Stay joined to me and let my teachings become part of you. Then you can pray for whatever you want, **and your prayer will be answered.** — *John 15:7 CEV*

15) Don't be like the people of this world, **but let God change the way you think. Then you will know how to do everything** that is **good** and **pleasing** to him. — *Romans 12:2 CEV*

16) At all times carry faith as a shield; for with it you will be able to put out all the burning arrows shot by the Evil One. ¹⁷And accept salvation as a helmet, **and the word of God as the sword which the Spirit gives you.** — *Ephesians 6:16-17 GNB*

17) Let the message about Christ completely fill your lives, while you use all your wisdom **to teach and instruct each other.** With thankful hearts, sing psalms, hymns, and spiritual songs to God. — *Colossians 3:16 CEV*

18) "This is the covenant that I will make with them in the days to come, says the Lord: **I will put my laws in their hearts and write them on their minds."** ¹⁷And then he says, "I will not remember their sins and evil deeds any longer." — *Hebrews 10:16-17 GNB*

19) We truly love God only when we obey him as we should, and then we know that we belong to him. — *1 John 2:5 CEV*

20) Nothing brings me greater happiness **than to hear that my children are obeying the truth.** — *3 John 1:4 CEV*

11d) Getting Sin Out of Your Lifestyle

Read On: March 9th | May 25th | August 10th | October 26th

1) He said, "If you will obey me completely by doing what I consider right and by keeping my commands, I will not punish you with any of the diseases that I brought on the Egyptians. I am the LORD, the one who heals you." — *Exodus 15:26 GNB*

2) You also must obey the LORD — you must worship him with all your heart and remember the great things he has done for you. — *1 Samuel 12:24 CEV*

3) You are always loyal to your loyal people, and you are faithful to the faithful. — *2 Samuel 22:26 CEV*

4) He told them: Faithfully serve the Lord! — *2 Chronicles 19:9 CEV*

5) You cannot be the slave of two masters! You will like one more than the other or be more loyal to one than the other. You cannot serve both God and money. — *Matthew 6:24 CEV*

6) Why do you keep on saying that I am your Lord, when you refuse to do what I say? — *Luke 6:46 CEV*

7) Jesus said to his disciples: If you love me, you will do as I command. — *John 14:15 CEV*

8) If you love me, you will do what I have said, and my Father will love you. I will also love you and show you what I am like. — *John 14:21 CEV*

9) If you obey me, I will keep loving you, just as my Father keeps loving me, because I have obeyed him. — *John 15:10 CEV*

10) I have told you this to make you as completely happy as I am. — *John 15:11 CEV*

11) The Spirit will come and show the people of this world the truth about sin and God's justice and the judgment. — *John 16:8 CEV*

189

12) What should we say? Should we keep on sinning, so that God's wonderful kindness will show up even better? ²No, we should not! If we are dead to sin, how can we go on sinning? — *Romans 6:1-2 CEV*

13) Dear friends, God is good. So I beg you to offer your bodies to him as a living sacrifice, pure and pleasing. That's the most sensible way to serve God. — *Romans 12:1 CEV*

14) God paid a great price for you. So use your body to honour God. — *1 Corinthians 6:20 CEV*

15) Someone will say, "I am allowed to do anything." Yes; but not everything is good for you. I could say that I am allowed to do anything, but I am not going to let anything make me its slave. — *1 Corinthians 6:12 GNB*

16) If we would examine ourselves first, we would not come under God's judgment. — *1 Corinthians 11:31 GNB*

17) Do not deceive yourselves; no one makes a fool of God. People will reap exactly what you sow. — *Galatians 6:7 GNB*

18) In the past you were dead because you sinned and fought against God. ²You followed the ways of this world and obeyed the devil. He rules the world, and his spirit has power over everyone who doesn't obey God. — *Ephesians 2:1-2 CEV*

19) Actually all of us were like them and lived according to our natural desires, doing whatever suited the wishes of our own bodies and minds. In our natural condition we, like everyone else, were destined to suffer God's anger. — *Ephesians 2:3 GNB*

20) But God's mercy is so abundant, and his love for us is so great, [5]that while we were spiritually dead **in our disobedience** he brought us to life with Christ. It is by **God's grace** that you have been **saved.** — *Ephesians 2:4-5 GNB*

21) Get rid of all **bitterness, passion,** and **anger.** No more **shouting** or **insults,** no more **hateful feelings** of any sort. — *Ephesians 4:31 GNB*

22) Whatever you say or do should be done in the name of the Lord Jesus, as you give thanks to God the Father because of him.
— *Colossians 3:17 CEV*

23) But if we confess our sins to God, he will keep **his promise** and do what is right: he will **forgive us our sins** and **purify us from all our wrongdoing.**
— *1 John 1:9 GNB*

24) Think how far you have fallen! Turn from your sins and do what you did at first. If you don't **turn from your sins,** I will come to you and take your lampstand from its place.
— *Revelation 2:5 GNB*

11e) Having Faith and
Trust in The Lord

Read On: March 10th | May 26th | August 11th | October 27th

1) After this, Abram had a vision **and heard the LORD say to him,** "Do not be afraid, Abram. **I will shield you from danger and give you a great reward.**"
— *Genesis 15:1 GNB*

2) The **Lord** is my Shepherd [to feed, guide, and shield me], **I shall not** lack. — *Psalm 23:1 AMP*

3) The LORD says, "I will teach you the way you should go; I will **instruct** you and **advise** you.
— *Psalm 32:8 GNB*

4) Be kind and bless us! **We depend on you.**
— *Psalm 33:22 CEV*

5) The sacrifice that honours me is a thankful heart. **Obey me, and I, your God, will show my power to save.** — *Psalm 50:23 CEV*

6) How great is God's love for all who worship him? Greater than the distance between heaven and earth!
— *Psalm 103:11 CEV*

7) The LORD is always kind to those who worship him, and he keeps his promises to their descendants. — *Psalm 103:17 CEV*

8) "Call to me, and I will answer you; I will **tell you wonderful** and **marvelous** things that you know nothing about. — *Jeremiah 33:3 GNB*

9) The LORD your God is with you; his power gives you victory. The LORD will take delight in you, and in his love he will give you new life. He will sing and be joyful over you. — *Zephaniah 3:17 GNB*

10) Take the yoke I give you. **Put it on your shoulders and learn from me.** I am gentle and humble, and you will find rest. — *Matthew 11:29 CEV*

Scripture Therapy Daily Devotional For Men

11) And He said to her, **Daughter, your faith (your trust and confidence in Me, springing from faith in God) has restored you to health.** Go in (into) peace and **be continually healed and freed from your [distressing bodily] disease.**
— *Mark 5:34 AMP*

12) from one generation to another **he shows mercy to those who honour him.**
— *Luke 1:50 GNB*

13) For **God so greatly loved** and dearly prized **the world** that He [even] gave up His only begotten (unique) **Son, so that whoever believes in (trusts in, clings to, relies on) Him shall not perish (come to destruction, be lost) but have eternal (everlasting) life.** — *John 3:16 AMP*

14) As the scripture says, **"Everyone who calls out to the Lord for help will be saved."** — *Romans 10:13 GNB*

15) However, as the scripture says: **"What no one ever saw or heard, what no one ever thought could happen, is the very thing God prepared for those who love him."**
— *1 Corinthians 2:9 GNB*

16) God has put all things **under the power of Christ, and for the good of the church** he has made him the **head of everything.** — *Ephesians 1:22 CEV*

17) Do all this **in prayer, asking for God's help. Pray on every occasion, as the Spirit leads.** For this reason keep alert and never give up; pray always for all God's people.
— *Ephesians 6:18 GNB*

18) The Lord will always keep me from being harmed by evil, and he will bring me safely into his heavenly kingdom. Praise him for ever and ever! Amen. — *2 Timothy 4:18 CEV*

19) So whenever we are in need, we should come bravely **before the throne of our merciful God.** There we will be treated with undeserved kindness, **and we will find help.** — *Hebrews 4:16 CEV*

20) **Let us hold on firmly to the hope we profess,** because **we can trust God** to keep his promise.
— *Hebrews 10:23 GNB*

22) **Obey God's message!** Don't fool yourselves by **just listening to it.** — *James 1:22 CEV*

21) No one can **please** God **without faith,** for **whoever comes** to God **must have faith** that **God exists** and **rewards** those **who seek him.** — *Hebrews 11:6 GNB*

11f) Being Faithful to Worship The Lord Daily

Read On: March 11th | May 27th | August 12th | October 28th

1) You are great and powerful, glorious, splendid, and majestic. Everything in heaven and earth is yours, **and you are king, supreme ruler over all.** — *1 Chronicles 29:11 GNB*

2) All the people of Judah were happy because they had made this **covenant** with all their heart. **They took delight in worshiping the LORD,** and he accepted them and **gave them peace** on every side. — *2 Chronicles 15:15 GNB*

3) I know that your goodness and love will be with me all my life; and your house will be my home **as long as I live.** — *Psalm 23:6 GNB*

4) Sing praise to the LORD, all his faithful people! **Remember what the Holy One has done, and give him thanks!** — *Psalm 30:4 GNB*

5) Then I will worship at your altar because you make me joyful. You are my God, and **I will praise you.** Yes, I will **praise you** as I play my harp. — *Psalm 43:4 CEV*

6) Giving thanks is the sacrifice that **honours me,** and I will surely save all who obey me." — *Psalm 50:23 GNB*

7) But I will sing about your strength, my God, and I will celebrate because of **your love.** You are my fortress, my place of protection in times of trouble. — *Psalm 59:16 CEV*

8) Your constant love is better than life itself, **and so I will praise you.** — *Psalm 63:3 GNB*

9) I will give you thanks as long as I live; I will **raise my hands** to you in prayer. — *Psalm 63:4 GNB*

10) My soul will feast and be satisfied, **and I will sing glad songs of praise to you.** — *Psalm 63:5 GNB*

11) Sing to the LORD, all the world! ²Worship the LORD with joy; come before him with happy songs! ³Acknowledge that the LORD is God. He made us, and we belong to him; we are his people, we are his flock. — *Psalm 100:1-3 GNB*

12) Enter the temple gates with thanksgiving; go into its courts with praise. Give thanks to him and praise him. ⁵The LORD is good; his love is eternal and his faithfulness lasts forever. — *Psalm 100:4-5 GNB*

13) O give thanks to the Lord, for He is good; for His mercy and loving-kindness endure forever. — *Psalm 136:1 AMP*

14) I will worship toward Your holy temple and praise Your name for Your loving-kindness and for Your truth and faithfulness; for You have exalted above all else Your name and Your word and You have magnified Your word above all Your name! — *Psalm 138:2 AMP*

15) Now those you have rescued will return to Jerusalem, singing on their way. They will be crowned with great happiness, never again to be burdened with sadness and sorrow. — *Isaiah 51:11 CEV*

16) Jesus answered: Love the Lord your God with all your heart, soul, and mind. — *Matthew 22:37 CEV*

17) I appeal to you therefore, brethren, and beg of you in view of [all] the mercies of God, to make a decisive dedication of your bodies [presenting all your members and faculties] as a living sacrifice, holy (devoted, consecrated) and well pleasing to God, which is your reasonable (rational, intelligent) service and spiritual worship. — *Romans 12:1 AMP*

18) In conclusion, be strong in the Lord [be empowered through your union with Him]; draw your strength from Him [that strength which His boundless might provides]. — *Ephesians 6:10 AMP*

19) Everything that God has created is good; nothing is to be rejected, but everything is to be received with a prayer of thanks, ⁵because the word of God and the prayer make it acceptable to God. — *1 Timothy 4:4-5 GNB*

11g) Victory Over The Power of
Your Enemy

Read On: March 12th | May 28th | August 13th | October 29th

1) Even if I go through the deepest darkness, I will not be afraid, LORD, for you are with me. Your shepherd's rod and staff protect me. — *Psalm 23:4 GNB*

2) All who belong to the LORD, show how you love him. The LORD protects the faithful, but he severely punishes everyone who is proud. — *Psalm 31:23 CEV*

3) You take care of everyone who loves you, but you destroy the wicked. — *Psalm 145:20 CEV*

4) My child, remember my teachings and instructions and obey them completely. ²They will help you live a long and prosperous life. — *Proverbs 3:1-2 CEV*

5) How can anyone break into a strong man's house and steal his things, unless he first ties up the strong man? Then he can take everything. — *Matthew 12:29 CEV*

6) Believers will be given the power to perform miracles: they will drive out demons in my name; they will speak in strange tongues. — *Mark 16:17 GNB*

7) I have given you the power to trample on snakes and scorpions and to defeat the power of your enemy Satan. Nothing can harm you. — *Luke 10:19 CEV*

8) The thief comes only in order to steal, kill, and destroy. I have come in order that you might have life — life in all its fullness. — *John 10:10 GNB*

9) in order to keep Satan from getting the upper hand of us; for we know what his plans are. — *2 Corinthians 2:11 GNB*

10) Christ obeyed God our Father and gave himself as a sacrifice for our sins to rescue us from this evil world. — *Galatians 1:4 CEV*

11) **Leave no [such] room** or foothold for the devil **[give no opportunity to him].** — *Ephesians 4:27 AMP*

12) We are not fighting against humans. We **are fighting against forces and authorities and against rulers of darkness and powers in the spiritual world.** — *Ephesians 6:12 CEV*

13) **At all times carry faith as a shield;** for with it you will be able to put out all the burning arrows **shot by the** Evil One. — *Ephesians 6:16 GNB*

14) **Don't be afraid of your enemies; always be courageous, and this will prove to them that they will lose and that you will win,** because it is God who gives you the victory. — *Philippians 1:28 GNB*

15) **God rescued us from the dark power of** Satan and brought us into the kingdom of his dear Son. — *Colossians 1:13 CEV*

16) For the Spirit that God has given us does not make us timid; **instead, his Spirit fills us with power, love, and self-control.** — *2 Timothy 1:7 GNB*

17) And then **they will come to their senses** and **escape from the trap** of the Devil, who had caught them and **made them obey his will.** — *2 Timothy 2:26 GNB*

18) **So be subject to God. Resist the devil [stand firm against him],** and he will **flee from you**. — *James 4:7 AMP*

19) **Be on your guard** and stay awake. **Your enemy,** the devil, is like a roaring lion, **prowling around to find someone to attack.** — *1 Peter 5:8 CEV*

20) I am writing to you, my children, **because you know the Father.** I am writing to you, fathers, because you **know him who has existed from the beginning.** I am writing to you, young people, because you are strong; **the word of God lives in you, and you have defeated** the Evil One. — *1 John 2:14 GNB*

21) But you belong to God, my children, and have **defeated the false prophets,** because **the Spirit who is in you is more powerful than the spirit in those who belong to the world.** — *1 John 4:4 GNB*

22) Every child of God can **defeat the world,** and **our faith is what gives us this victory.** — *1 John 5:4 CEV*

23) We know that none of God's children keep on **sinning, for the Son of God keeps them safe, and the** Evil One **cannot harm them.** — *1 John 5:18 GNB*

CHAPTER 12

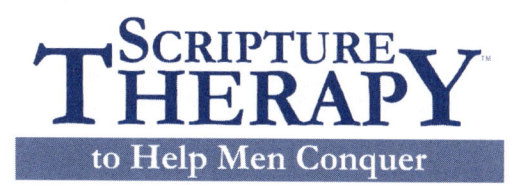

Scripture Therapy™ to Help Men Conquer Lawful Behaviour Issues

TOPICS

12a) Abiding by The Law at All Times
Read On: March 13th | May 29th | August 14th | October 30th

12b) Living a Life of Obedience to God's Commands
Read On: March 14th | May 30th | August 15th | October 31st

12c) Getting Rid of Your Bad Behaviour
Read On: March 15th | May 31st | August 16th | November 1st

12d) Being a Law-Abiding Citizen
Read On: March 16th | June 1st | August 17th | November 2nd

12e) Getting Rid of a Criminal Lifestyle
Read On: March 17th | June 2nd | August 18th | November 3rd

12a) Abiding by The Law
At All Times

Read On: March 13th | May 29th | August 14th | October 30th

1) Be patient and trust the LORD. **Don't let it bother you when all goes well for those who do sinful things.** — *Psalm 37:7 CEV*

2) Teach me, LORD, what you want me to do, and I will obey you faithfully; teach me to serve you with complete **devotion**. — *Psalm 86:11 GNB*

3) Your **insight** and **understanding** will **protect** you [12]**and prevent you from doing the wrong thing.** They will keep you away from people who stir up trouble by what they say. — *Proverbs 2:11-12 GNB*

4) **The** LORD **doesn't like anyone who is dishonest,** but he lets **good people** be his friends. — *Proverbs 3:32 CEV*

5) He places a **curse** on the home of everyone who is **evil, but he blesses the home of every good person.** — *Proverbs 3:33 CEV*

6) **The** LORD **sneers at those who sneer at him,** but he is **kind** to everyone who is **humble**. — *Proverbs 3:34 CEV*

7) **The lifestyle of good people** is like sunlight at dawn that **keeps getting brighter** until broad daylight. — *Proverbs 4:18 CEV*

8) **Sinners are trapped and caught by their own evil deeds.** — *Proverbs 5:22 CEV*

9) **If you respect the** LORD**, you will hate evil.** I hate **pride** and conceit and **deceitful** lies. — *Proverbs 8:13 CEV*

10) **If you obey the** LORD**, you won't go hungry; if you are wicked, God won't let you have what you want.** — *Proverbs 10:3 CEV*

11) **If you live right, the reward is a good life;** if you are **evil,** all you have is sin. — *Proverbs 10:16 CEV*

Scripture Therapy Daily Devotional For Men

12) What evil people dread most will happen to them, **but good people will get what they want most.** *— Proverbs 10:24 CEV*

13) Wise friends make you wise, but you hurt yourself **by going around with** fools. *— Proverbs 13:20 CEV*

14) A young man who obeys the law is intelligent. One who makes friends with good-for-nothings is a **disgrace to his father.** *— Proverbs 28:7 GNB*

15) Honesty will keep you safe, but everyone who is **crooked will suddenly fall.** *— Proverbs 28:18 CEV*

16) If you are foolishly boasting or planning something evil, then stop it now! *— Proverbs 30:32 CEV*

18) Now we know that everything in the Law applies to those who live under the Law, in order to stop all human excuses and bring the whole world under God's judgment. *— Romans 3:19 GNB*

17) Because everyone will do what is right, there will be peace and security forever. *— Isaiah 32:17 GNB*

19) Everyone must obey the state authorities, because no authority exists without God's permission, and the existing authorities have been put there by God. *— Romans 13:1 GNB*

20) People who oppose the authorities are opposing what God has done, and they will be punished. *— Romans 13:2 CEV*

21) Don't fool yourselves. **Bad friends will destroy you.** *— 1 Corinthians 15:33 CEV*

23) Rendering service readily with goodwill, **as to the LORD and not to men,** ⁸Knowing that for **whatever good anyone does, he will receive his reward from the LORD,** whether he is slave or free. *— Ephesians 6:7-8 AMP*

22) Leave no [such] room or foothold for the devil [give no opportunity to him]. *— Ephesians 4:27 AMP*

12b) Living a Life of Obedience to God's Commands

Read On: March 14th | May 30th | August 15th | October 31st

1) But God will never **abandon the faithful** or ever give help to evil people. — *Job 8:20 GNB*

2) Even those who are guilty will be forgiven, **because you obey God.** — *Job 22:30 CEV*

3) LORD, who may enter your Temple? Who may worship on Zion, your sacred hill? ²Those who obey God in everything and always do what is right, whose words are true and sincere. — *Psalm 15:1-2 GNB*

4) Happy is the one whom the LORD does not accuse of doing wrong and who is free from all deceit. — *Psalm 32:2 GNB*

5) Righteous people — people of integrity — will live in this land of ours. — *Proverbs 2:21 GNB*

6) Always let him lead you, and he will clear the road for you to follow. — *Proverbs 3:6 CEV*

7) When God is angry, money won't help you. Obeying God is the only way to be saved from death. — *Proverbs 11:4 CEV*

8) You can be sure of this: All crooks will be punished, but God's people won't. — *Proverbs 11:21 CEV*

9) God cannot stand the prayers of anyone who disobeys his Law. — *Proverbs 28:9 CEV*

10) The LORD blesses everyone who is afraid to do evil, but if you are cruel, you will end up in trouble. — *Proverbs 28:14 CEV*

11) Anyone who can be trusted in little matters can also be trusted in important matters. But anyone who is dishonest in little matters will be dishonest in important matters. — *Luke 16:10 CEV*

12) Dear friends, **God is good.** So I beg you to offer your bodies to him as a living sacrifice, **pure and pleasing.** That's the most sensible way to serve God.
— *Romans 12:1 CEV*

13) Then you will be the pure and innocent children of God. You live among people who are crooked and evil, **but you must not do anything that they can say is wrong.** Try to shine as lights among the people of this world,
— *Philippians 2:15 CEV*

14) Whatever you do, **work at it with all your heart, as though you were working for the** LORD **and not for human beings.** ²⁴Remember that the LORD will give you **as a reward** what he has **kept for his people.** For **Christ** is the real Master you **serve.** — *Colossians 3:23-24 GNB*

15) Make it your aim to live a quiet life, to mind **your own business,** and to earn **your own living,** just as we told you before.
— *1 Thessalonians 4:11 GNB*

16) Dear friends, **you must never become tired of doing right.**
— *2 Thessalonians 3:13 CEV*

17) Do your best to win full approval in God's sight, as a worker who is **not ashamed of his work,** one who **correctly teaches** the message of God's truth.
— *2 Timothy 2:15 GNB*

18) If anyone makes himself or herself clean from all those evil things, they will be used for **special purposes,** because they are **dedicated** and **useful** to their Master, **ready to be used** for every good deed. — *2 Timothy 2:21 GNB*

19) He preferred to suffer with God's people rather **than to enjoy sin for a little while.** — *Hebrews 11:25 GNB*

20) When we love others, **we know that we belong to the truth, and we feel at ease in the presence of God.** — *1 John 3:19 CEV*

21) **God is love, and anyone who doesn't love others** has never known him. — *1 John 4:8 CEV*

22) No one has ever seen God. But if we love each other, **God lives in us, and his love is truly in our hearts.** — *1 John 4:12 CEV*

23) **Love means that we do what God tells us.** And from the beginning, he told you to love him. — *2 John 1:6 CEV*

24) I know what you do; I know that you have a little power; **you have followed my teaching and have been faithful to me. I have opened a door in front of you, which no one can close.** — *Revelation 3:8 GNB*

12c) Getting Rid of
Your Bad Behaviour

Read On: March 15th | May 31st | August 16th | November 1st

1) The LORD hates evil thoughts, but kind words please him. — *Proverbs 15:26 CEV*

2) If you want to **stay out of trouble, be careful what you say.** — *Proverbs 21:23 GNB*

3) I looked for someone to **defend the city** and to **protect it from my anger**, as well as to stop me from destroying it. **But I found no one.** — *Ezekiel 22:30 CEV*

4) What should we say? **Should we keep on sinning, so that God's wonderful kindness will show up even better?** ²No, we should not! If we are dead to sin, how can we go on sinning? — *Romans 6:1-2 CEV*

5) He will go ahead of the LORD with the same power and spirit that Elijah had. And because of John, **parents will be more thoughtful of their children. And people who now disobey God will begin to think as they ought to.** That is how John will get people ready for the LORD. — *Luke 1:17 CEV*

6) But you do not live as your human nature tells you to; instead, you **live as the Spirit tells you to** — if, in fact, God's Spirit lives in you. Whoever does not have the Spirit of Christ does not belong to him. — *Romans 8:9 GNB*

7) Don't be like the people of this world, **but let God change the way you think.** Then you will know **how to do everything that is good and pleasing to him.** — *Romans 12:2 CEV*

8) Work hard and do not be lazy. **Serve the LORD with a heart full of devotion.** — *Romans 12:11 GNB*

9) Let us conduct ourselves properly, as people who live in the light of day — **no orgies or drunkenness, no immorality or indecency, no fighting or jealousy.** — *Romans 13:13 GNB*

10) **Come back to your right senses and stop your sinful ways.** I declare to your shame that some of you do not know God.
— *1 Corinthians 15:34 GNB*

11) Your life must be controlled by love, just as **Christ loved us and gave his life for us** as a sweet-smelling offering and sacrifice that pleases God. — *Ephesians 5:2 GNB*

12) Everything in the **Scriptures** is God's Word. **All of it is useful for teaching and helping people and for correcting them and showing them how to live.** — *2 Timothy 3:16 CEV*

13) The **Scriptures train God's servants to do all kinds of good deeds.**
— *2 Timothy 3:17 CEV*

14) As for us, we have this large crowd of witnesses around us. So then, **let us rid ourselves of everything that gets in the way, and of the sin which holds on to us so tightly,** and let us run with determination the race that lies before us. — *Hebrews 12:1 GNB*

15) **Stop being hateful!** Stop trying to fool people, and start being sincere. **Don't be jealous or say cruel things about others.**
— *1 Peter 2:1 CEV*

16) Be on your guard and stay awake. Your enemy, the devil, is like a roaring lion, **prowling around to find someone to attack.** — *1 Peter 5:8 CEV*

17) If we [freely] admit that we have sinned and confess our sins, He is **faithful** and just (true to His own nature and promises) **and will forgive our sins** [dismiss our lawlessness] and [continuously] **cleanse us from all unrighteousness** [everything not in conformity to His will in purpose, thought, and action]. — *1 John 1:9 AMP*

18) When we obey **God,** we are sure that we know him.
— *1 John 2:3 CEV*

19) We truly love God only when **we obey him as we should,** and then we know that we belong to him.
— *1 John 2:5 CEV*

20) I am writing to you, my children, because you know the Father. I am writing to you, fathers, because you know him who has existed from the beginning. I am writing to you, young people, **because you are strong; the word of God lives in you, and you have defeated the Evil One.**
— *1 John 2:14 GNB*

21) Don't love the world or **anything that belongs to the world. If you love the world, you cannot love the Father.**
— *1 John 2:15 CEV*

22) Our foolish pride comes from this world, **and so do our selfish desires and our desire to have everything we see.** None of this comes from the Father. — *1 John 2:16 CEV*

23) None of those who are children of God continue to sin, for God's very nature is in them; and because God is their Father, **they cannot continue to sin.** — *1 John 3:9 GNB*

24) From the beginning you were told **that we must love each other.**
— *1 John 3:11 CEV*

12d) Being
A Law-Abiding Citizen

Read On: March 16th | June 1st | August 17th | November 2nd

1) But God will **snatch the wicked from the land** and **pull sinners out of it like plants** from the ground. — *Proverbs 2:22 GNB*

2) There are seven things that the Lord hates and cannot tolerate: **A proud look, a lying tongue, hands that kill innocent people,** a mind that thinks up wicked plans, feet that hurry off **to do evil,** a witness who tells one lie after another, and someone who **stirs up trouble among friends.** — *Proverbs 6:16-19 GNB*

3) The Lord hates anyone who cheats, but he likes **everyone who is honest.** — *Proverbs 11:1 CEV*

4) **Trouble goes right past the Lord's people** and strikes the wicked. — *Proverbs 11:8 CEV*

5) **If good people are rewarded here on this earth,** all who are **cruel and mean** will surely be punished. — *Proverbs 11:31 CEV*

6) **Follow the road to life,** and **you won't be bothered** by death. — *Proverbs 12:28 CEV*

7) **Showing respect to the Lord will make you wise,** and being humble **will bring honour to you.** — *Proverbs 15:33 CEV*

8) Lawbreakers praise criminals, but **law-abiding citizens** always oppose them. — *Proverbs 28:4 CEV*

9) From that time Jesus began to preach his message: **"Turn away from your sins, because the Kingdom of heaven is near!"** — *Matthew 4:17 GNB*

10) Do not let evil defeat you; instead, **conquer evil with good.** — *Romans 12:21 GNB*

11) Everyone must obey the state authorities, because no authority exists without God's permission, and the existing authorities have been put there by God. — *Romans 13:1 GNB*

12) People who oppose the authorities are opposing what God has done, and they will be punished. — *Romans 13:2 CEV*

13) In the past you were spiritually dead because of your disobedience and sins. — *Ephesians 2:1 GNB*

14) At that time you followed the world's evil way; you obeyed the ruler of the spiritual powers in space, the spirit who now controls the people who disobey God. — *Ephesians 2:2 GNB*

15) And become useful and helpful and kind to one another, tenderhearted (compassionate, understanding, loving-hearted), forgiving one another [readily and freely], as God in Christ forgave you. — *Ephesians 4:32 AMP*

16) Do as God does. After all, you are his dear children. — *Ephesians 5:1 CEV*

17) Jesus Christ will keep you busy doing good deeds that bring glory and praise to God. — *Philippians 1:11 CEV*

18) and don't have anything to do with evil. — *1 Thessalonians 5:22 CEV*

19) In the name of the LORD Jesus Christ we command these people and warn them to lead orderly lives and work to earn their own living. — *2 Thessalonians 3:12 GNB*

20) And then they will come to their senses and escape from the trap of the Devil, who had caught them and made them obey his will. — *2 Timothy 2:26 GNB*

21) And let our own [people really] learn to apply themselves to good deeds (to honest labor and honorable employment), so that they may be able to meet necessary demands whenever the occasion may require and not be living idle and uncultivated and unfruitful lives. — *Titus 3:14 AMP*

22) Don't fall in love with money. Be satisfied with what you have. The Lord has promised that he will not leave us or desert us. — *Hebrews 13:5 CEV*

23) But be doers of the Word [obey the message], and not merely listeners to it, betraying yourselves [into deception by reasoning contrary to the Truth]. — *James 1:22 AMP*

24) Surrender to God! **Resist** the devil, and he will run from you. — *James 4:7 CEV*

25) If our conscience **condemns us, we know that God is greater than our conscience** and that he knows everything. — *1 John 3:20 GNB*

12e) Getting Rid of
A Criminal Lifestyle

Read On: March 17th | June 2nd | August 18th | November 3rd

1) Hear me, LORD, when I call to you! Be merciful and answer me! — *Psalm 27:7 GNB*

2) Happy are those whose sins are forgiven, whose wrongs are pardoned. — *Psalm 32:1 GNB*

3) When I did not confess my sins, I was worn out from crying all day long. ⁴Day and night you punished me, LORD; my strength was completely drained, as moisture is dried up by the summer heat. ⁵Then I confessed my sins to you; I did not conceal my wrongdoings. I decided to confess them to you, and you forgave all my sins. — *Psalm 32:3-5 GNB*

4) Don't give in to worry or anger; it only leads to trouble. — *Psalm 37:8 GNB*

5) When they call to me, I will answer them; when they are in trouble, I will be with them. I will rescue them and honour them. — *Psalm 91:15 GNB*

6) We may think we are doing the right thing, but the LORD always knows what is in our hearts. — *Proverbs 21:2 CEV*

7) Doing what is right and fair pleases the LORD more than an offering. — *Proverbs 21:3 CEV*

8) My children, you must respect the LORD and the king, and you must not make friends with anyone who rebels against either of them. — *Proverbs 24:21 CEV*

9) It's better to be poor and live right, than to be rich and dishonest. — *Proverbs 28:6 CEV*

10) If you don't confess your sins, you will be a failure. But God will be merciful if you confess your sins and give them up. — *Proverbs 28:13 CEV*

11) The **thief** comes only in order to **steal, kill, and destroy. I have come** in order that **you might have life — life in all its fullness.** — *John 10:10 GNB*

12) "Peace is what I leave with you; it is my own peace that I give you. I do not give it as the world does. **Do not be worried and upset; do not be afraid.**" — *John 14:27 GNB*

13) "Happy are those **whose wrongs are forgiven,** whose sins are **pardoned!**" — *Romans 4:7 GNB*

14) The night is nearly over, day is almost here. **Let us stop doing the things that belong to the dark,** and let us **take up weapons** for fighting in the light. — *Romans 13:12 GNB*

15) But clothe yourself with the LORD **Jesus Christ** (the Messiah), **and make no provision for [indulging] the flesh [put a stop to thinking about the evil cravings of your physical nature]** to [gratify its] desires (lusts). — *Romans 13:14 AMP*

16) Some of you say, "We can do anything we want to." **But I tell you that not everything is good for us.** So I refuse to let anything **have power over me.** — *1 Corinthians 6:12 CEV*

17) My friends, God has made us these promises. **So we should stay away from everything that keeps our bodies and spirits from being clean.** We should honour God and try to be completely like him. — *2 Corinthians 7:1 CEV*

18) If you are a thief, stop stealing. Be honest and work hard, so you will have something to give to people in need. — *Ephesians 4:28 CEV*

19) Those who used to rob must stop robbing and start working, in order to earn an honest living for themselves and to be able to help the poor. — *Ephesians 4:28 GNB*

20) Put on all the armour that God gives you, **so that you will be able to stand up against the** Devil's **evil tricks.** — *Ephesians 6:11 GNB*

21) Let your faith be like a shield, and you will be able to **stop all the flaming arrows** of the evil one. — *Ephesians 6:16 CEV*

22) He rescued us from the power of darkness and brought us safe into the kingdom of his dear Son. — *Colossians 1:13 GNB*

23) Let us then **fearlessly** and **confidently** and **boldly draw near to the throne of grace** (the throne of God's unmerited favor to us sinners), **that we may receive mercy [for our failures]** and find **grace to help in good time** for every need [appropriate help and well-timed help, coming just when we need it]. — *Hebrews 4:16 AMP*

24) My brothers and sisters, consider yourselves fortunate when all kinds of trials come your way, ³**for you know that when your faith succeeds in facing such trials,** the result is the ability to endure. — *James 1:2-3 GNB*

25) So then, **submit to God.** Resist the Devil, and he will **run away from you.** — *James 4:7 GNB*

Other Books By
Scripture Therapy Resources

Scripture Therapy
Daily Devotional
for **Men**

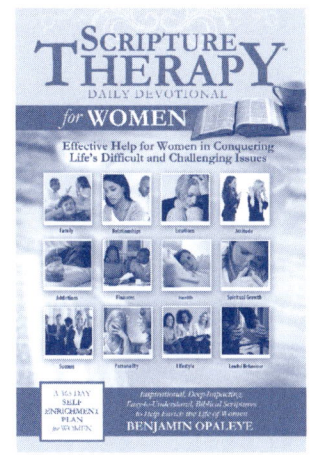

Scripture Therapy
Daily Devotional
for **Women**

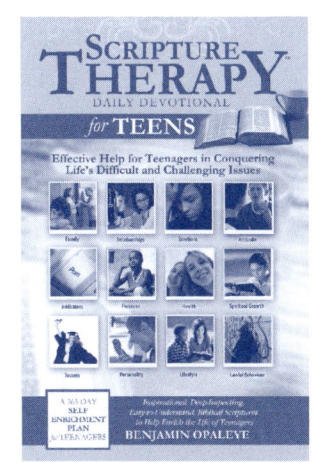

Scripture Therapy
Daily Devotional
for **Teens**

Scripture Therapy
Daily Devotional
for **Children (8-12)**

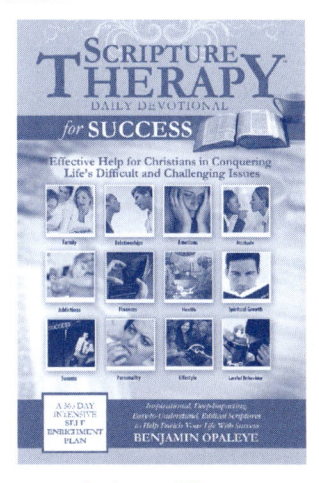

Scripture Therapy
Daily Devotional
for **Success**

For new and upcoming releases visit our website at
www.ScriptureTherapy.com

TESTIMONIES

Dear reader,

If this devotional has been a blessing to you or someone you know we would love to hear from you.

Kindly share your testimony with us using the space provided below.
Detach and send to:
Scripture Therapy Resources
P. O. Box 68475
London N16 1EJ
UK

Or email it to: Testimonies@ScriptureTherapy.com

.... DETACH HERE ....

MY TESTIMONY _____
_____
_____
_____
_____
_____
_____
_____
_____
_____
_____
_____
_____
_____

Name: _____
Email Address: _____
Phone (Optional): _____